ESSENTIAL PROVISIONS

Essential PROVISIONS

Beliefs, Virtues, & Practices For The Spiritual Journey

CENTRALPRESS
Ministry Resources from
Central Bible Church

Printed in the United States of America
ISBN: 979-8-811-43980-5

Published by Central Press
Central Bible Church
8001 Anderson Boulevard
Fort Worth, Texas 76120
www.wearecentral.org

First Printing 2022

This book is dedicated to Dr. Tom Bulick, Pastor of Spiritual Formation at Central Bible Church since 1998. During that time, he has produced more than 1,000 editions of The Scrolls, *a weekly Bible Study. Tom's commitment to God's Word and his use of the Core Competencies in his writings have impacted generations of disciples.*

CONTENTS

CENTRAL PRACTICES

Preface

I joined the pastoral staff of Central Bible Church (formerly Pantego Bible Church) in August of 1998 after serving as Vice President for Student Life and Associate Professor of Religious Studies at Trinity Western University in Langley, BC Canada for twelve years. I desired to return to church ministry, and my wife Ruth, son Zach, and I were attracted to this church by its intentional strategy for disciple-making, which included among other things, a mission focused on spiritual transformation and the 31 Core Competencies—10 Core Beliefs, 10 Core Practices, and 11 Core Virtues.

For these past 24 years I have had the pleasure of employing the 31 Core Competencies through my weekly writing of *The Scrolls* and teaching of Community Group Bible Study at Central Bible Church. Many of you reading this devotional have been encouraged by the Competencies through your own personal use of *The Scrolls* or through your children's engagement with them on Sunday mornings. The Core Competencies have served us well as a church in our mission of "making God known by making disciples who are changed by God to change their world." Here are three specific ways the Competencies have been a helpful tool for disciple-making at Central Bible Church.

First, the Competencies serve as a description of mission accomplishment. It's one thing to have a mission. It's quite another to have a clear vision of what its fulfillment looks like. The Core Competencies provide this vision and an implicit strategy for attaining it. The strategy assumes that a growing comprehension of the 10 Core Beliefs coupled with an increasingly frequent, more consistent engagement in the 10 Core Practices is used by the Holy Spirit to develop the 11 Core Virtues, the benchmarks of a maturing disciple of Christ (Galatians 5:22-23).

Second, the Competencies serve as a curriculum for mission accomplishment. It follows that if these doctrines, disciplines, and character qualities picture mission fulfillment, then they ought to be taught. In the beginning, they served as a lectionary of sorts. Sermons were developed *around* the Competencies. That pattern was adjusted after a few years and replaced by matching a particular Core Competency to the biblical text chosen.

Third, the Competencies give people a common language to use to discuss Christian theology and spiritual formation. As such, they serve as a biblical theology of spiritual formation intended to increase the biblical and theological literacy of Christ's disciples.

As you work through the 31 Core Competencies in this devotional, I pray you will gain not only a greater understanding of them, but also a deeper appreciation for how they help form us into more fully developed followers of Christ.

Tom Bulick, PhD
March 2022

Introducing the Core Competencies

If you aim at nothing, you'll hit it every single time. Unfortunately, this is the default of much spiritual living. Call it "incidental transformation." A person goes to church a few Sundays each month, has a group of Christian friends that they regularly associate with, and may even be a regular listener to a podcast of a well-known ministry leader. Whatever life-change they experience is incidental—almost accidental. They weren't aiming for any growth objective and, therefore, they aren't necessarily conscious of the impact their church, community, podcast, or any number of things might or might not have on their life.

Contrast this common experience with "intentional transformation." This person is aware of undeveloped aspects of their spiritual life and wishes to mature as a disciple of Jesus. The Apostle Paul urges Christians toward this conscious pursuit,

> Therefore, my dear friends, as you have always obeyed—not only in my presence, but now much more in my absence—continue to work out your salvation with fear and trembling, for it is God who works in you to will and to act according to his good purpose. (Philippians 2:12-13)

Much of this chapter is adapted from *Next Step Discipleship: The Christian's Handbook for Walking the Pathway to Missional Living*, by David Daniels, ©2016, Central Press. This book describes the Spiritual Pathway used at Central Bible Church.

The Philippians could no longer count on Paul's spoon-feeding and would need to intentionally attend to their salvation—or sancitification—in his absence. Spiritual growth is cultivated in community and through various activities. But, each Christian is personally responsible to join the Holy Spirit in this lifelong pursuit.

The Core Competencies give the Christian something to aim at. They do not form a complete list of Christian beliefs, virtues, and practices. But, they are "core" or central. Let's take a moment and better understand each set of competencies.

CENTRAL BELIEFS

Knowledge is what a disciple understands to be true. Before belonging to Jesus Christ, people neither seek truth nor understand truth (Romans 3:11). Because they do not possess the Holy Spirit, they cannot understand spiritual things (1 Corinthians 2:14). The Bible describes this condition as "foolishness"—being dull to the wisdom and ways of God. In fact, the fool denies the existence of God, despises correction, hates instruction, is impulsive in passions and decisions, speaks proudly and is bent on destruction (Psalm 14:1-2).

However, when a person turns to the Lord, he gives them his Holy Spirit who, in turn, gives them the "mind of Christ" (1 Corinthians 2:12, 16). With this new spiritual disposition, the Christian is able to "grow in the knowledge of the Lord," increasing understanding of God and his ways (Colossians 1:10, 2 Peter 3:18). Though the accumulation of knowledge may be nothing more than the mere appearance of maturity for some people (1 Corinthians 8:1), for the truly mature it is the foundation for their spiritual zeal (Proverbs 19:2, Romans 10:1-3). As they read God's Word, they desire, understand and apply spiritual truth that sets them free (John 8:32).

The Bible, in its 66 books, is filled with life-changing truth. But in a limited discipleship relationship, there are some truths that must take priority for the growing believer. At Central Bible Church, we refer to Central Beliefs—essential truths that every Christian must understand. Many of these competencies were originally proposed in *The Connecting Church,* by Pastor Randy Frazee. Since then, Central Bible Church has modified the list to the following Central Beliefs:

Authority of the Bible
Church
Eternity
The Holy Spirit
Humanity
Identity in Christ
Jesus Christ
Life Purpose
Personal God
Salvation by Grace

CENTRAL VIRTUES

Virtue, or character, is what a disciple becomes. It refers to the inner virtues cultivated by the Holy Spirit. As a believer is conformed to the image of Jesus, they think and talk and act like Jesus—the proof of a heart increasingly transformed. Peter describes this change in 2 Peter 1:3-8,

> His divine power has given us everything we need for life and godliness through our knowledge of him who called us by his own glory and goodness. Through these he has given us his very great and precious promises, so that through them you may participate in the divine nature and escape the

> corruption in the world caused by evil desires. For this very reason, make every effort to add to your faith goodness; and to goodness, knowledge; and to knowledge, self-control; and to self-control, perseverance; and to perseverance, godliness; and to godliness, brotherly kindness; and to brotherly kindness, love. For if you possess these qualities in increasing measure, they will keep you from being ineffective and unproductive in your knowledge of our Lord Jesus Christ.

Several spiritual principles are stated in this powerful passage. First, God, through his Spirit, has provided every Christian what we need to live a godly life. Second, according to the promise of God, we are able to "participate in the divine nature"—becoming like Jesus—and escape the corruption of the world (see also Romans 12:1-2). Third, since we have this potential, we should intentionally "add to" our faith all of the virtues mentioned. Finally, as our character is conformed to Christ, we become productive and effective in our life with Jesus.

Character is essentially the "overflow of the heart." The Christian wants to be loving, gracious, merciful and kind at the core. But, even before the believer experiences this inward change, they can choose to act according to these and other character traits. Very often, the Bible commands the Christian to show love, be gracious, act mercifully or treat people with kindness, with the expectation that as they cooperate with the Holy Spirit, they will learn to be what they do. In other words, their actions will form their character.

Like knowledge, there are dozens of character traits that God wishes to refine in the Christian. The following 11 Central Virtues are especially important:

Gentleness
Grace

Faithfulness
Hope
Humility
Joy
Kindness/Goodness
Love
Patience
Peace
Self-Control

CENTRAL PRACTICES

Practices are what a disciple can do. These are the skills or aptitudes of the spiritual life. Just as a child learns how to walk, ride a bike, or drive a car with age, so the Christian develops skills that help their spiritual growth and make them more fruitful in their service to God. Historically, many skills have been called "disciplines" of the spiritual life. As opposed to "works" that people do to gain favor with God, disciplines are healthy spiritual habits inspired by grace. They are practices that overflow from a person's relationship with God.

Just as the vision, knowledge and character mentioned above are normative for the Christian, so these skills should be normative as well. If I were invited to someone's home for a meal and they were feeding their 13-year-old son, I would form one of two conclusions: Their son was lazy or their son had a developmental difficulty that prevented him from being able to feed himself. Similarly, we must conclude that Christians who do not pray, share their faith, or practice financial stewardship, for example, are either lazy or spiritually deficient. A growing disciple becomes increasingly proficient at spiritual skills.

Like the other competencies, there are dozens of skills that God wishes to develop in the Christian. The following 10 Central

Practices are especially important:

Bible Study
Biblical Community
Compassion
Disciple-Making
Evangelism
Generosity
Prayer
Single-Mindedness
Spiritual Gifts
Worship

No doubt, the reader will ask, "But, what about _____?" and will wonder about some foundational truth, some character trait, or some skill not mentioned in these lists. Where is the imminent return of Jesus, or faith, or fasting? Remember that none of the lists are intended to be exhaustive. They are foundational. More important is that the disciple has a list—a core set of essential truths, virtues, and disciplines that become the focus of their spiritual development.

Each of the brief chapters that follow will give the reader a snapshot of one Core Competency. Included is a credal statement that summarizes the competency and a key verse from Scripture. No doubt, the reader may identify more meaningful texts to support any competency. The goal here is not to be complete, but to highlight specific dimensions of the spiritual life where the maturing disciple may focus their attention. Hopefully, this little book will sharpen your aim.

CENTRAL BELIEFS

AUTHORITY OF THE BIBLE

I believe the Bible is the Word of God and has the right to command my belief and action.

"All Scripture is God-breathed and is useful for teaching, rebuking, correcting, and training in righteousness, so that the man of God may be thoroughly equipped for every good work."
2 Timothy 3:16-17

Michael Novak, a Roman Catholic philosopher, once shared in an address the problem with our public education system in America: "They teach, 'There is no such thing as truth. Truth is bondage. Believe what seems right to you. There are as many truths as there are individuals. Follow your feelings. Do as you please. Get in touch with yourself. Do what feels comfortable.'" Unfortunately, it is safe to say that many people today hold a similar understanding of truth. A significant reason why this is the case is that so few people have any ultimate authority in their life to determine what truth is.

As God's people we have determined that God's Word will be the ultimate authority in our lives because we believe that Scripture is set apart and inspired. Here is how Central Bible Church's Statement of Faith explains the uniqueness and authority of the Bible: "We believe literally in the Scriptures of the Old and New Testaments as inspired of God, inerrant in the original writings, and of supreme and final authority in faith and life."

Second Peter 1:20-21 provides our rationale for this belief, "knowing this first of all, that no prophecy of Scripture comes from someone's own interpretation. For no prophecy was ever produced by the will of man, but men spoke from God as they were carried along by the Holy Spirit."

We can be confident that the Bible is our ultimate authority in life by looking at four elements central to this belief:

Inspiration – Source of Authority

All Scripture is God-breathed (2 Timothy 3:16-17). The more than 40 authors of Scripture, spanning over 1600 years, were moved by God's Spirit using their own style, vocabulary, and experience. The resulting writings were not their words alone, but the very words of God. Because of its divine inspiration, we adhere to the belief that God's Word is superior to all other ideas or ideologies.

Infallibility/Inerrancy – Authentication of Authority

The Bible is perfect and complete because God is perfect and complete (Titus 1:2; Hebrews 6:18) and without falsehood or error (Matthew 5:17-18). Scripture in the original manuscripts does not affirm anything that is contrary to fact. Think of this: If you believed the Bible was filled with error in one area, could you still trust what God said in any other area?

Inclusion – Limitation of Authority

At the Council of Carthage (AD 397), the biblical canon (the set of all the books that belong in the Bible) was established. The Church did not choose which books should be canon, but rather, they officially recognized the authority of the books as inspired by God. The main qualification for determining which books were Scripture was whether they had evidence of divine authorship. You can rest easy; there are no battles for any canonical change today.

Interpretation – Application of Authority

The Bible is necessary for knowing the gospel, maintaining spiritual life, and knowing God's will for our lives. John 10:27 says, "My sheep hear my voice, and I know them, and they follow me." As we consider Scripture's authority in our lives, we might ponder on these questions: If we believe the Bible to be authoritative, do we live like it? What if you treated your Bible like your phone, checking it for messages at the beginning and end of the day? Can you say that when you read the Bible, you hear the voice of God speaking to you in a way that is true of no other book?

PRAYER

Father, I want your inspired Word to guide my life as the ultimate authority. Help me to know it more because I want to know you more. Help me to hide your Word in my heart, that I might not sin against you (Psalm 119:11). Amen.

CHURCH

I believe the church is God's primary way to accomplish his purposes on earth today.

"Instead, speaking the truth in love, we will in all things grow up into him who is the Head, that is, Christ. From him the whole body, joined and held together by every supporting ligament, grows and builds itself up in love, as each part does its work."
Ephesians 4:15-16

We believe in the Church. It might sound a little strange for a church to say they believe in the Church. What we mean is that we hold a deep conviction that one of God's foundational pieces of his work and movement in the world, across all of history, is in his creation of the Church. The Lord's Church has purpose and design, and as Christ-followers we are woven into those plans. This is especially important for us to understand today for a couple of reasons. One, the definitions and distinctions of what the Church is and is intended to be are seemingly so widely varied. For instance, should a church function solely in the virtual world? Two, our culture is increasingly seeing the Church as irrelevant to their lives. A recent Gallup poll revealed that for the first time in their 80 years of reviews, fewer than half (47%) of Americans identified with any church or house of worship of any faith. Many people today are asking what the Church is about and whether it really matters to them.

There are two strong word pictures in the Scriptures for the

Church. They help us understand God's plan for the Church and our place within it.

The Church Is a Bride

As the redeemed of Christ, we are corporately the Bride and Jesus is our Groom. Revelation 19:7 reads that "the marriage of the Lamb has come, and his Bride has made herself ready." This is a picture of the intimate love that is ours in Christ. Jesus is as devoted, passionate, and committed to us as his Church as a groom is to his wife. Christ has pursued, drawn, and wooed us. He will never leave us. We are forever welcomed. As the Bride, we are to be true to our love, devoted and secure. The Church as a bride is about who we are. It defines our identity. We are loved. We belong to Christ.

The Church Is a Body

We not only have an identity as the Church as a bride, but we also have a purpose as a body. "Just as a body, though one, has many parts, but all its many parts form one body, so it is with Christ. For we were all baptized by one Spirit so as to form one body—whether Jews or Gentiles, slave or free—and we were all given the one Spirit to drink. Even so the body is not made up of one part but of many" (1 Corinthians 12:12-14). Every Christ-follower has a unique purpose within the Church, within God's plans. We have each been fitted with spiritual giftings "to equip his people for works of service, so that the body of Christ may be built up until we all reach unity in the faith and in the knowledge of the Son of God and become mature, attaining to the whole measure of the fullness of Christ" (Ephesians 4:12-13). As a body, the Church finds its purpose and meaning. There is a calling on our life.

PRAYER

Father, you are the architect of the Church. You have designed it and given it meaning. The Church expresses the deep love you have for me. You have loved me as a Bride, with great faithfulness and care. May I open myself even more today to your love, and secure myself in who you say I am. You have gifted me and called me to a place within the body of the Church. You've given me purpose, a unique way to love and serve the world around me in your name. May I spend myself for your glory in the Church. Amen.

ETERNITY

I believe there is a heaven and a hell, and that Jesus Christ is returning to judge the earth and to establish his eternal kingdom.

"Do not let your hearts be troubled. Trust in God; trust also in me. In my Father's house are many rooms; if it were not so, I would have told you. I am going there to prepare a place for you. And if I go and prepare a place for you, I will come back and take you to be with me that you also may be where I am. You know the way to the place where I am going."
John 14:1-4

John Lennon's signature song, "Imagine," was released in 1971 as a plea for world peace. His lyrics describe what he imagined life would be like without eternity.

Imagine there's no heaven
It's easy if you try
No hell below us
Above us only sky
Imagine all the people living for today
Imagine there's no countries
It isn't hard to do
Nothing to kill or die for
And no religion too
Imagine all the people living life in peace
You may say I'm a dreamer
But I'm not the only one

Lennon seemed to believe that if he could somehow—by the power of his own imagination—erase God and eternity, then people would live only for today. This, he thought, would result in world unity and peace among all of mankind. However, history has shown that Lennon's dream of a Godless society lived for the here and now always results in a nightmare.

With no hope of a God caring for us who will one day set all things right, no larger meaning or purpose in life, no reliable standards for behavior, and no truly long-term consequences to consider, people often turn to despair, self-medicating, looking for their identity in things that will never satisfy, seeking power through harmful means, or simply putting themselves above others to make sure their own desires or personal needs are met.

Thankfully, the Bible declares that God has made us for eternity. He has even placed a longing for heaven in our hearts (Ecclesiastes 3:11).

Let's consider three biblical truths about eternity:

Eternity Happens Now and Later

Often when we think of eternity, we think of a never-ending timeline that begins once we experience physical death or upon the return of Jesus. In truth, eternity is something that will happen later, but it is also something happening now. Every person alive today and every person who has ever lived is experiencing some form of eternity. We are eternal beings.

Eternity Is Experienced by Everyone, but Not Everyone Will Experience the Same Eternity

All who are in Christ will experience eternal life in and with Jesus, while those who reject Jesus will experience eternal punishment and separation from his presence. Jesus said, "Then they will go away to eternal punishment, but the righteous to eternal life" (Matthew 25:46). Though the world rejects this theology, the Bible is crystal clear about both God's gracious reward to those who trust Christ and God's righteous judgment on those who reject him.

Eternity Brings Hope to Those Who Have Eternal Life

As believers we are experiencing eternal life now, but we also live with great expectation of being glorified with Christ in the future. Colossians 3:4 reads, "When Christ, who is your life, appears, then you also will appear with him in glory." When times are tough in this life, we often remind ourselves that this is not the end of the story. One day we will find ourselves face-to-face with the Lord and justice will be served. Suffering and sickness will no longer wage war on our bodies. Peace and unity will be all that we know. This promise of eternity enables us to hold on in hope and persevere through trials.

PRAYER

Father, thank you for the abundant gift of eternal life that you have given me in Jesus. Help me to live a life that advances your eternal kingdom. Give me the opportunity to share the reason for the hope you have given me with those who are still dead in their sins. In Jesus' name, Amen.

HOLY SPIRIT

I believe the Holy Spirit convicts, calls, converts and changes me as a child of God.

"You, however, are not in the realm of the flesh but are in the realm of the Spirit, if indeed the Spirit of God lives in you. And if anyone does not have the Spirit of Christ, they do not belong to Christ."
Romans 8:9

One of the most beautiful expressions of God's love for us is his act of adopting us as sons and daughters into his family. Paul writes about this beautiful relationship in his letter to the Romans when he says we are assured by the Holy Spirit that we are children of God (Romans 8:14-16). The Holy Spirit is the sealing gift given to those who believe in Jesus and receive salvation.

This precious and powerful gift of the Holy Spirit in my life is evident in so many ways. I recognize that the Spirit of God drew me to the Lord and convicted me of my own sin and desperate need for salvation. The Spirit guided me to the truth of the gospel and produced a changed heart in me. He works in me daily to bring me closer to Jesus and to be shaped to be more like him. He makes me aware of the path he wants me to take in my life. He encourages me through his Word and through my fellowship with other disciples to live out God's calling to make disciples of all nations by expressing Christian love to all people.

The Holy Spirit is constantly at work in my life. This is true for all Christians as evidenced in Scripture and in times of personal reflection. Following are six ways that the Holy Spirit is at work in a believer's life. Reflect on the reality of his work in your own life in the following ways.

He Convicts

The Holy Spirit comes upon the world to convict people of sin, righteousness, and judgment. He convicts people concerning the sin of unbelief in Jesus Christ the Savior, the righteousness necessary for those who would spend eternity with the Lord, and the reality that judgment has come upon Satan, who has already been defeated (John 16:8-11). Conviction such as this demands a response leading to transformation necessary for eternal life with God. Without conviction, humans are destined to live a hopeless and idolatrous life that leads to eternal suffering and separation from God.

He Converts

The Holy Spirit works to transform the human who, only through the work of God, hears the gospel and responds in belief. The Holy Spirit also cleanses us from sin, regenerating us and declaring us righteous (Titus 3:4-7). Without conversion, one cannot enter the perfect, unblemished family of God. Only through God's grace is this transformation possible. The proper response of the one converted is devotion to doing good according to the Lord's general and specific calling.

He Calls

The Holy Spirit empowers each believer with gifts that are to be used for the common good (1 Corinthians 12:7). The general calling of the Lord for Christians is to utilize those gifts within their righteous lives, living according to their new life created in Christ Jesus for good works (Ephesians 2:10). It is constantly observed that the Holy Spirit of God calls specific people to specific work to be done according to the will and plans of the Father. From Old Testament patriarchs and matriarchs to New Testament apostles, the chosen people of God are specifically called and empowered by the Holy Spirit to do certain things and pursue a certain mission. Thankfully, the Lord does not leave us to fulfill our general or specific calling alone. The Lord promises that he will be with us as we pursue him and live out his calling in our lives (Matthew 28:20).

He Changes

The Holy Spirit, from his wooing of our heart to the fulfillment of the calling in the earthly life of each Christian, is cleansing us from sin and making each of us more holy. This transforming work of the Holy Spirit, also known as sanctification, is for the ultimate purpose of elevating the glory of the Lord as we recognize and thank him for his beautiful and constant formation of our hearts (2 Corinthians 3:18). Christians speak often about the desire to be more like Jesus. The reality is that sanctification is not possible without the consistent work of the Holy Spirit in the hearts of those who call Jesus Lord.

He Comforts

Before Jesus died, he promised his disciples that he would not leave them to be alone, but would ask the Father to give them a Comforter and Advocate, the Holy Spirit, who would be with them forever and bring them his peace (John 14:16, 26-27). The Holy Spirit also goes before us to the Father and intercedes for us when we do not know what to pray for (Romans 8:26).

He Counsels

The Holy Spirit counsels through the Word of God to illuminate truth and guide God's people in the right paths. He reminds us of who Jesus is and what he has done on our behalf (John 16:13-15). He even helps us when we do not know what to say or how to act in our gospel encounters. In fact, he tells us not to worry about what to say but to trust him, knowing that the Spirit of the Father will speak through us (Matt 10:19-20).

PRAYER

Father, thank you for the glorious grace that you have lavished upon me. Thank you for saving me and generously giving me the gift of the Holy Spirit in my life. Lord, by your Spirit help me to be more like Jesus. I know that I cannot be the person you want me to be apart from your Spirit's constant work of transformation in my life. I submit to you, Father, and to the ministry of your Holy Spirit. In the name of Jesus and by the power of your Spirit I pray. Amen.

HUMANITY

I believe all people are loved by God and need Jesus Christ as their Savior.

"For God so loved the world that he gave his one and only Son,
that whoever believes in him shall not perish but have eternal life."
John 3:16

The creed describing the Central Belief Humanity contains two assertions: one, that all people are loved by God, and two, that all people need Jesus Christ as their Savior. Let's reflect on them in reverse order. The Bible says that all people need Jesus Christ as their Savior because "There is no one righteous" (Romans 3:10), or put the other way around, because "all have sinned" (v. 23). So on the one hand, no one is morally perfect, and on the other, everyone is morally flawed. Ironically, people who are reluctant to call themselves "sinners" commonly admit they're imperfect. Ask someone, "Are you a sinner?" and you may hear them answer, "I wouldn't call myself a sinner. But I wouldn't call myself religious either. I do, however, think I'm a spiritual person, and I try to follow the Golden Rule."

Ask the same person, "Are you morally perfect?" and you will no doubt hear them answer, "Of course not; no one is morally perfect." In fact, people often confess but then excuse their moral shortcomings by adding, "After all, nobody's perfect."

Logically, the biblical fact that all have sinned does not imply moral equivalence. In other words, just because Hitler is a sinner and Mother Teresa is a sinner that doesn't mean they are morally the same. Otherwise, there would be no need for future judgment. While all "fall short of the glory," that is, the moral perfection, "of God" (Romans 3:23), some fall farther short than others.

The Bible also says that God loves all people, namely, the same people who need Jesus Christ as their Savior. John 3:16, perhaps the most familiar verse in the Bible, reads, "For God so loved the world that he gave his one and only Son, that whoever believes in him shall not perish but have eternal life." By the term "world," the apostle means all people without exception, that is, every single human being, not just all kinds of people without distinction—Jews, Gentiles, men and women, rich and poor. Of course, if the first proposition is true, the second is as well. John confirms this in 1 John 2:2. Speaking of Jesus Christ, he writes, "He is the atoning sacrifice for our sins," namely, all those who believe, "and not only for ours but also for the sins of the whole world," namely, all those who do not believe.

It is best to avoid the contemporary tendency to describe God's love in romantic terms. God loves the world; he is not madly in love with the world. The magnitude of his love is not found in the strength of God's emotion but in the infinite worth of Christ's sacrifice. The hymn "The Love Of God" by Frederick Lehman and Claudia Mays puts it best:

Could we with ink the ocean fill,
And were the skies of parchment made;
Were every stalk on earth a quill,
And every man a scribe by trade;
To write the love of God above,
Would drain the ocean dry;

Nor could the scroll contain the whole,
Though stretched from sky to sky.

PRAYER

Father, strengthen me so that I, together with all of your holy people, might grasp how wide and long and high and deep is the love of Christ and know this love that surpasses full comprehension (Ephesians 3:14-19). Amen.

IDENTITY IN CHRIST

I believe I am significant because of my position as a child of God.

"Yet to all who received him, to those who believed in his name, he gave the right to become children of God."
John 1:12

"Who are you?" This is a fundamental question that everyone must answer at some point in their life. What makes you… you? Are you defined by your looks, your marital status, or your career? Do you find your value in how many likes you get on your Facebook posts? Does your identity change based on the decisions you make, or your successes and your failures?

Someone once wrote in an article in *Psychology Today*, "Identity may be acquired indirectly from parents, peers, and other role models. Children come to define themselves in terms of how they think their parents see them. Psychologists assume that identity formation is a matter of 'finding oneself' by matching one's talents and potential with available social roles." Are you what others think of you? Or are you the summation of your talents and your ability to perform some meaningful role in this world?

As a people who believe in God as the Author of life, we look to our Creator to determine our fundamental identity. An artist takes a lump of clay, molds it, shapes it, and forms it into the image that he desires. Our identity was determined by the One who made us. Genesis 1:26 tells us, "Then God said, 'Let us make mankind in our image, in our likeness, so that they may rule over the fish in the sea and the birds in the sky, over the livestock and all the wild animals, and over all the creatures that move along the ground.'" Our fundamental identity, our value, and our significance are not up for grabs. They were defined by God. We were created in God's image for his perfect purposes, to represent him and to rule and reign on earth as his representatives.

But as we know, something went terribly wrong. Man and woman rebelled against their Creator (Genesis 3), and that perfect identity became marred and malformed—distorted from God's original design. The sin of Adam brought death to us all (Romans 5:12). That death is most evidenced in our separation from the Author of life. Sin created a chasm between us and God that we could never bridge by ourselves.

Thankfully, God had plans to bridge this great divide himself. Because of his great love for us, God sent his Son to not only perfectly bear his image, but also to rescue us from our sin through his death and resurrection. Christ died as our substitute so that we might be forgiven and restored to our God. Ephesians 2:8-9 says, "For it is by grace you have been saved, through faith—and this is not from yourselves, it is the gift of God—not by works, so that no one can boast." He did it all! We cannot add to his perfect sacrifice for our sin. When we trust in Jesus, the Bible tells us that we take on a new identity—Christ's identity. Now the Father sees us as he sees the One who perfectly embodied his image. By God's grace, this is who we are as his children.

So, what now?

1. Rejoice and be glad! (Philippians 4:4)

2. Thank God and give him the praise he deserves! (Psalm 139:14)

3. Grow in intimacy with him! (Psalm 34:4)

4. Serve him with all your heart! (Joshua 24:15)

5. Share this Good News with those who are searching for their significance! (John 17:20-24)

PRAYER

Father, thank you for creating me and calling me to yourself through your Son, Jesus Christ. My heart rejoices because through Jesus, you have given me the right to be called a child of God (John 1:12). Draw me to a more intimate walk with you, to know your love in deeper ways. Let me serve you all the days of my life and share the Good News of Christ to those who are desperately searching for their significance. In Jesus' name I pray. Amen.

JESUS CHRIST

I believe Jesus Christ is the Son of God who became man, died for sinners and rose from the dead.

"In the past God spoke to our forefathers through the prophets at many times and in various ways, but in these last days he has spoken to us by his Son, whom he appointed heir of all things, and through whom he made the universe. The Son is the radiance of God's glory and the exact representation of his being, sustaining all things by his powerful word. After he had provided purification for sins, he sat down at the right hand of the Majesty in heaven. So he became as much superior to the angels as the name he has inherited is superior to theirs."
Hebrews 1:1-4

The Bible is filled with hundreds of stories with hundreds of people, a cast of major and minor characters. But no one is more important than Jesus. In fact, he stands centerstage, all the spotlights of the Bible pointing to him. The Old Testament anticipates Jesus, and the New Testament celebrates him.

The Central Belief of Jesus Christ affirms both his identity and his ministry. First, Jesus is the Son of God. He was more than just a good man; Jesus was the God-man. Jesus is God who came to earth to live among us. The deity of Jesus is confirmed throughout the Scriptures in key passages such as Philippians 2:5-11 and Hebrews 1:1-4. However, some of the most compelling evidence comes from Jesus himself.

First, Jesus said that he was God. Jesus said, "I and the Father are one" (John 10:30) and "Anyone who has seen me has seen the Father" (John 14:9). Several times, when Jesus expressed his deity, his hearers threatened to stone him—the Jewish penalty for making oneself equal with God (see John 8:58-59; Mark 14:61-64).

Second, Jesus believed he was God. He accepted worship from others (Matthew 9:18), claimed the authority to forgive sins (Mark 2:5), and announced that all judgment was given into his hands (John 5:22).

Someone can *claim* to be God and simply be lying, a charlatan out to take advantage of others. Someone could *believe* themselves to be God and simply be a lunatic, terribly deceived. But, Jesus went the distance and *proved* he was God. He healed the sick, restored sight to the blind, preached with heavenly authority, did not sin, and rose from the dead! The irrefutable proof of Jesus' identity assures us that God's Son came to live among us. And this confirmed identity of who Jesus was makes what Jesus did so incredible. God rescued sinners!

God loved the world so much that he sent his Son to bring us to himself. The love of God is shown in Jesus' incarnation. That is, Jesus left his glorious place in heaven and stooped to become mere flesh and blood. He humbly became like us in order to take our place. God's love continues in Jesus' crucifixion. Jesus carried the sins of the world and absorbed the wrath of God that each of us deserves. Finally, God's love is revealed in Jesus' resurrection—Jesus raised to new life, a guarantee that people can be born again into a new life with God.

The question everyone must ask is, "What will I do with Jesus?" If God has come to you, have you come to God? Jesus' life, death, and resurrection is an invitation to a personal and eternal relationship with the living God. We accept this invitation through faith—believing in who Jesus was and what Jesus did. Don't turn another page without pausing to give Jesus your sin and receiving his gift of new life. Jesus, the Son of God, offers the only way to life with God forever (John 14:6).

PRAYER

Father, thank you for your unfailing love, shown to me in your Son Jesus. You didn't have to save me, but you sacrificed your own Son so that I could be forgiven and free. I believe that Jesus is your Son and that he lived, died, and rose from the grave. I believe that salvation isn't possible by any other means than faith in Jesus. So, I trust him. And I ask that you would make me more like Jesus, my Savior. Amen.

LIFE PURPOSE

I believe I am a steward of God's resources and have been redeemed to participate in his kingdom purposes for his glory.

"However, I consider my life worth nothing to me; my only aim is to finish the race and complete the task the Lord Jesus has given me—the task of testifying to the good news of God's grace."
Acts 20:24

In a conversation with the Cheshire Cat, Alice (from *Alice in Wonderland*) asked, "Would you tell me please, which way I ought to go from here?" "That depends a good deal on where you want to get to," said the cat. "I don't much care where," said Alice. "Then it doesn't matter which way you go," said the cat.

Often, I find Christians without purpose are a little like Alice. I see many people who don't really understand their purpose as they walk through life. Perhaps you have felt the same way. Maybe you are stuck in the monotony of work, or maybe you are going through the motions with your spouse or family. Perhaps you feel that life has lost meaning, and you are resigned to the idea that you are "going nowhere." There's good news for you: God has something in store for you that is greater than you might have imagined!

God is the only one qualified to define and give us life purpose. He created life and he created us. Doesn't it stand to reason that he has the right to give us purpose? Ephesians 2:10 helps to clarify three truths about God's purpose for our lives.

The verse begins by stating in the Greek that "we are God's masterpiece!" This is a special statement indeed! Have you ever thought of yourself as a masterpiece? I love this statement, because not only does it speak to the worth God places on us, but it also indicates the extent to which God is involved with us. He is 100% bought into you and me! This is the first great truth we need to wrap our minds around. He isn't interested in us merely a few days each year or even each month. He is completely bought into us fulfilling the purposes that he has set before us. How can we be sure he is this bought into us? Just look what he gave up for us all. Our lives are worth the blood of Christ, his Son. If that's not "all in," I don't know what is!

But God doesn't stop there—he continues in Ephesians 2:10 saying that we are "created in Christ Jesus to do good works, which God prepared in advance for us to do." This is good news for us, because God is the one who is setting the agenda. This second truth is foundational. God knows how we fit into the team in the best way. He knows how we are gifted, and he desires for us to be stewards of what he gives us and participate in his Kingdom purposes.

The final truth brings this all together: God brings about the fulfillment of these purposes as we walk with him. A better translation of the last part of Ephesians 2:10 is, "which God prepared in advance for us to walk in them." This makes the point that we are to walk in good works. What does that mean? To walk in good works is to walk by faith in God and to trust that as we walk with him, God will work through us. God is the one who is at work in us but also through us. Not only does he set the purpose, he also fulfills that purpose through us as we walk close to him! Is there a better deal than that?

Take some time today to thank the Lord that he is bought into you, that he is setting the course for your life, and that he is helping you accomplish the purposes he is setting. Always remember that "he who began a good work in you will carry it on to completion until the day of Christ Jesus" (Philippians 1:6).

PRAYER

Dear God, help me to put aside my agenda and my plans. Please reveal to me the purpose you have for my life. May I be a good steward of the time and resources you have given me. I ask you to work in me to impact others for the sake of the gospel. Amen.

PERSONAL GOD

I believe God is involved in and cares about my daily life.

"I lift my eyes to the hills – where does my help come from?
My help comes from the LORD, the Maker of heaven and earth."
Psalm 121:1-2

In Genesis 24, aging Abraham sends his most trusted servant in search of a wife for his beloved son, Isaac. After a long journey, the servant sits near a well where he boldly and specifically prays for God to give him success. Before he is even finished with his prayer, lovely Rebekah appears. She's clearly the bride he was sent to find, and the servant is utterly overwhelmed with how God answered his prayer. At dinner, he won't take one bite of food until he marvels at the Lord, "Let me tell you what my God has done!"

How Do You View God?

The servant clearly had a high view of God that saw him as being engaged in the affairs of man. When I was young, I thought of God in two different ways—one, a cosmic genie pulling strings and yelling at people, and the other, a man in the sky who winds us up and sends us on our own way to fend for ourselves. Today, my view of God is vastly different. The Lord is almighty, gracious, everlasting, unchanging, powerful, holy, compassionate, righteous, and the list goes on and on, exploding the conceptions of my finite mind and dropping me to my knees in awe. God is alive and active, wooing and calling us into a deeper relationship with him. The one who created the universe and everything in it desires to be in relationship with you. With all your faults, brokenness, and shortcomings, he cares about you deeply.

How Is Your Relationship with God?

The man that Abraham chose to go on this significant mission showed devotion and reverence. He pursued his task with wisdom and diligence, calling on the Lord for success. His prayer wasn't a cry for help in a moment of desperation—rather it showed an abiding and trusting relationship with a faithful God. Any good relationship is likely a result of effort and intentionality. Is God what you do on Sunday but the rest of the week he gets put on the shelf? He has more to offer than that. Jeremiah 29:13—"You will seek me and find me, when you seek me with all your heart." How are you seeking God? When do you spend time with him? Is your relationship with the Lord growing?

Are You Allowing God Into the Dark Places in Your Life?

I imagine the enormity of the servant's task and the pending consequence of failure. I wonder if he thought he was up for the job ahead or if he'd rather have passed it to someone more qualified. There have been times in my life when difficult situations and circumstances began to pile on like bricks so that I felt I was carrying the weight of the world with no end in sight. During a time of great trouble and distress, I remember taking each day step by step, clinging to God's Word and promises. You might be in that spot right now. God sees you. He knows every detail of what's happening in your world. He's right beside you, hurting with you and offering comfort. Do you know how much he loves you?

When Are You Celebrating His Goodness?

We often get caught in the loop of wake up-work-family-bed on repeat each day without truly acknowledging and sharing God's goodness. Like the servant, I don't want to take a bite of food without recognizing what God is doing in my life and testifying to his glory. What is God doing in your life and how are you sharing this with others?

PRAYER

Lord, when I consider all you are—Creator, Sustainer, Ruler over all—I'm humbled and amazed that you pursue me. Father, you hung the stars in the sky and command the waves, yet love me personally with gentleness and kindness. "Create in me a pure heart, O God, and renew a steadfast spirit within me" (Psalm 51:10). Help me to desire you more, seeking and celebrating you in all circumstances. Amen.

SALVATION BY GRACE

I believe a person comes into a right relationship with God by His grace, through faith in Jesus Christ.

"For by grace you have been saved, through faith—and this is not from yourselves, it is the gift of God—not by works, so that no one may boast."
Ephesians 2:8-9

One day before our first child was born, my wife and I had a conversation about whether we would involve Santa Claus in our Christmas gift-giving with our kids. I was taking the No Santa position, but not for the reason most people would think. I didn't want Santa involved because I didn't want him to get the credit for the biggest and best gifts on Christmas morning. I wanted the extra love and attention that would come when I presented my daughter with her first bike or the play kitchen she really wanted. What started out as a goofy conversation revealed in me a desire for recognition and reason to boast in what I could offer others. I wanted my daughter to think I was a great dad because of what I gave her.

In one way or another, this is a mindset that rings true for most of us. We want credit and recognition for what we do. However, when it comes to the things of God we are called to boast only in our weaknesses (2 Corinthians 12:10) and remember that God began the work of salvation. God, and God alone, should receive the glory, the pride, and the celebration. Our right standing with the Father (justification) has nothing to with us but instead has everything to do with the generous and loving God of the Bible. The same God who sent his Son to be a propitiation for our sins, who laid down his life, ultimately reigns victorious over sin and death. We need to realize that our salvation is rooted in the graciousness of God alone and not graciousness and our works.

As we seek to live in a constant remembrance of our salvation by the grace of God, I want to give you a few reminders to cling to in your spiritual life.

Salvation by Grace Reminds Us of Who We Were

Most can very easily remember times when we were distant from the things of God, but it's important to remember that regardless of how far along we are in the Christian journey, we have a testimony that reminds us of our past struggles, difficulties, and sin habits. During those struggles or sin habits, we turned to Jesus and trusted that he could fix the brokenness and make us whole. We offered him nothing, but He gave us everything (Ephesians 2:5).

Salvation by Grace Reveals to Us Who We Are

When we placed our faith in Jesus, we became more aware of and sensitive to the things of God. Things that were once incredibly foreign and strange became things that we desired because we wanted to be obedient to God. We no longer have to live according to the flesh and its desires; we are free to walk in a life that is shared with Jesus as his disciples and children of his kingdom (Ephesians 2:6-7).

Salvation by Grace Revitalizes Us in Our Daily Lives

When we are able to live our lives free from the fear of a merit-based salvation, we are free to live in a manner worthy of our calling. We no longer fear the outcome but instead seek to glorify God and his kingdom in all that we do. Instead of boasting in our accomplishments, we boast in the Lord and his faithfulness. God gets the glory and God gets the recognition.

PRAYER

Father, thank you for all that you have done to secure my salvation with you. Thank you for sending Jesus and for the life he lived, the death he died, and his resurrection that ensured our victory. You are such a gracious God, and I acknowledge that you alone are enough for my salvation. I surrender to your will and desire to be obedient to you. Amen.

CENTRAL VIRTUES

FAITHFULNESS

I have established a good name with God and with others based on my long-term loyalty to those relationships.

"Let love and faithfulness never leave you; bind them around your neck, write them on the tablet of your heart. Then you will win favor and a good name in the sight of God and man."
Proverbs 3:3-4

In recent months, I have been struck with the desire to do more. A need arises, and I want to help above and beyond. A ministry shares their vision, and I yearn to give above and beyond. A venture opportunity presents itself, and I desire to be involved above and beyond. In every one of these instances and many more, I have felt God gently nudging me, saying, "Be faithful where you are."

Maybe you can relate with the idea of wanting to do more. I catch myself often staring at the green grass on the other side of the fence and dreaming about doing more. My prayers look like this, "God, if you only give me more, I will give more," or "If you give me greater influence, I can lead more people to Christ and godly living." These might sound self-serving, and perhaps there is an element of that, but even in my purest moments when I deeply desire to do the most for the Kingdom, I sense God tenderly reminding me: "Be faithful where you are."

One of my favorite passages in the Bible is the Parable of the

Talents in Matthew 25. Three servants are given a portion of money. One servant received $5000, one servant received $2000, and one servant received $1000. The first two servants put their portions to good use and doubled the amount they were given. The last servant went and buried his portion. In the end, the master returned to collect what he had given his servants. The last servant was rebuked for sitting on what he was given, but the first two were commended. The master blessed the first two servants saying, "Well done, good and faithful servant! You have been faithful with a few things; I will put you in charge of many things. Come and share your master's happiness!" (Matthew 25:21). Even though the portions given to the first two servants were different, their commendations were the same. So then, the rewards of the master have nothing to do with the results we produce, but rather with the faithfulness with which we steward that which he has given us.

I have often thought, why would the last servant (also called the lazy servant) do nothing with his portion? Why go and bury it or sit on it? I wonder if he looked at what others had and simply thought, "If only I had that portion, of course I could do much more." His analysis led to paralysis.

Allow me to suggest two steps to cultivate faithfulness: Gratitude and Initiative. The Lord doesn't have to bless us, but he does. Perhaps take a moment to list all the good things in your life. Start with the things you take for granted. Gratitude takes the focus off of others and what they have. It helps us to recognize and be thankful for all God has given us. Then, with a grateful attitude take the initiative to use what God has given you to be a blessing to others. Ask the question: What can I do with what God has given me? Then make it more specific: What can I do with my ability to play guitar? What can I do with my Spanish? What can I do with my extra time each Tuesday night? And continue to remember that God simply asks us to be faithful where we are.

PRAYER

Dear Father, please help me to take my eyes off of others and to be thankful for all you have given me. Would you help me to use all you have given me for your glory? Help me to live in such a way that at the end of my life, you would say to me, "Well done, good and faithful servant! You have been faithful with a few things; I will put you in charge of many things. Come and share your master's happiness!" Amen.

GENTLENESS

I am thoughtful, considerate, and calm in dealing with others.

"Let your gentleness be evident to all. The Lord is near."
Philippians 4:5

Gentleness is easy when everyone is getting along and everything is going your way. It's much more difficult in situations in which your patience is greatly tried; even more challenging if you're being treated unjustly. In those moments, gentleness is seen for what it truly is—a supernatural expression of the Spirit of God resident in a person. It reminds me of Jesus' prayer for his persecutors as they were fastening him to a cruel instrument of death: "Father, forgive them, for they know not what they do" (Luke 23:34). Christ could have easily brought a quick end to those soldiers and the godless empire they represented. However, he responded with incredible meekness toward their wicked treatment. How could Jesus act with such gentleness? First Peter 2:23 explains: "When he was reviled, he did not revile in return; when he suffered, he did not threaten, but continued entrusting himself to him who judges justly." Jesus could show such gentleness because he completely trusted in God's sovereign care and justice. He didn't have to fight for himself. You don't have to fight for yourself either.

In this "age of outrage" in which we live, gentleness is often in short supply. Let me suggest four ways to cultivate this fruit of the Spirit in your life:

Abide in Christ

Jesus said, "abide in me" and you'll "bear much fruit" (John 15). Gentleness is an overflow of Christ living in us through his Spirit and Word. Jesus declared that he is "gentle and lowly in heart" (Matthew 11:29). Read and meditate on Scripture daily, even throughout your day, to drink deeply of God's life-transforming elixir of gentleness.

Adjust Your Expectations

If we expect life to run smoothly, gentleness will be far more difficult to express. So, expect delays in your schedule. Understand that your children are going to disobey at times. Remind yourself that machines are built to break. Smile at life's interruptions because Jesus sits on his throne.

Amass Gentle Friends

Proverbs 22:24 says, "Make no friendship with a man given to anger." The people we spend time with greatly influence our behavior. This includes the music on our playlist, the personalities in our feeds, and the talking heads that gain our attention. Surround yourself with Christlike meekness in both your embodied friends and your virtual "friends."

Ask for It!

Our Father in heaven desires that we walk by the Spirit and not by the flesh. When we ask him to grow gentleness in our lives, it is his desire to answer that prayer.

PRAYER

Father, grant me the gentleness of Christ that others may see you through my life. Empower me to be an ambassador of peace with such confidence in my King that meekness is my response to the various forms of opposition I encounter in this life. Lead me to love those who reject me and to show kindness in the face of anger. Help me to "walk in a manner worthy of the calling to which [I] have been called, with all humility and gentleness, with patience, bearing with one another in love" (Ephesians 4:1-2). Amen.

GRACE

I demonstrate forgiveness, mercy, and generosity to others, even when they have offended me.

"Bear with each other and forgive one another if any of you has a grievance against someone. Forgive as the Lord forgave you."
Colossians 3:13

Imagine having a coworker who constantly messes up. They're regularly late, they miss deadlines, they're consistently inconsistent, and they're overall difficult to work with. One morning you walk into the office to see their desk has been cleared. You reasonably assume that they've been fired, but to your bewilderment, you learn that they've been promoted to an executive position that includes a pay raise. How would you feel?

Nobody minds when people get what they deserve. Good people earn good things, and bad people earn bad things; it's only fair. But what about when someone gets something they haven't earned? It seems natural to call "foul" in such situations, but believers in God ought to appreciate such a situation better than anyone. When we get what we don't deserve, we're recipients of grace. We should be regularly reminding ourselves of God's grace toward us as we grow in our faith.

Here are a few helpful things to remember as we consider what grace is:

Grace Is Necessary

Scripture tells us in Romans 3:23 that "all have sinned and fall short of the glory of God." We are, by virtue of being born into a fallen world, sinners; all of us are born with a debt we owe. Likewise, everyone has failed to uphold the law of God at some point. Scripture tells us that "the wages of sin is death" (Romans 6:23). Thankfully, though, God paid that debt through the person of Jesus so that we can be fully redeemed.

Grace Is Free

God sent his son Jesus to pay the debt of sin for anyone who would believe (John 3:16). Because Jesus was without sin he was able to adequately pay the cost of sin for the world (2 Corinthians 5:21). In doing so, he provided a path to righteousness for anyone who places their faith in him. The Bible says, "all are justified freely by his grace through the redemption that came by Christ Jesus" (Romans 3:24).

Grace Is for Sharing

When we act graciously to others we honor God. In fact, God's expectation is that those who are recipients of his grace would demonstrate it to others. We're told to "be merciful just as your Father is merciful" (Luke 6:36) and to let our speech "always be gracious" (Colossians 4:6). We're told to clothe ourselves with "compassion, kindness, humility, gentleness, and patience" and to "forgive as the Lord forgave" us (Colossians 3:12-13). Grace given to us is meant to be shown through us.

Life will never be short on moments when someone wrongs us. Our sinful world is unsurprisingly filled with sinners. But when Christians choose to extend grace to someone who has wronged them, and we forfeit our right to be angry, we give a broken world a glimpse of the perfect love that is in Christ Jesus.

PRAYER

God, thank you for your grace that never runs out. Thank you for demonstrating your love for me through the sacrifice of Jesus. As I embrace today, I ask your Spirit to show me ways I can demonstrate grace to others. Help me to earnestly forgive others, to speak kindly to everyone I encounter, and to be increasingly patient when I experience trials. I pray that in my demonstrations of grace you will be glorified, I will be encouraged, and a hurting world will be brought closer to you. Amen.

HOPE

I can cope with the hardships of life and with death because of the hope I have in Jesus Christ.

"We have this hope as an anchor for the soul, firm and secure. It enters the inner sanctuary behind the curtain, where Jesus, who went before us, has entered on our behalf."
Hebrews 6:19-20

Many people know that the average human body can only survive about a month without food, even less without water. However, have you ever wondered how long someone can live without hope? Hope, like food and water, is essential for human life. In many respects, the object of our hope becomes a source of life for us. Ultimately, what we place our hope in provides us meaning and purpose. But what happens if the object of our hope is not steady and secure? If I place my hope in my money, what becomes of my identity when the stock market crashes? If my hope is anchored to my career, what happens to my sense of purpose when I am let go or demoted?

Jesus alone is worthy of our hope because he alone is faithful and unchanging. He alone will never let us down. Listen to what Romans 5:3-5 says: "We can rejoice, too, when we run into problems and trials, for we know that they help us develop endurance. And endurance develops strength of character, and character strengthens our confident hope of salvation. And this hope will not lead to disappointment. For we know how dearly God loves us, because he has given us the Holy Spirit to fill our hearts with his love." Hope in Christ never leads to disappointment!

A few weeks ago, I officiated the wedding of my only sibling's only child, Faith. As she came down the aisle with my brother, I was filled with joy and jubilation. My mind went back to about 25 years ago when on the fairway of the first hole of golf, I asked my brother what he and my sister-in-law were going to do after several years of struggling with a bleak infertility diagnosis and multiple disappointments. His response was, "We're just going to trust God. We think he has a plan." Even when there was good reason to be overtaken by doubt, they had a seed of hope deep in their hearts. Hence, the name give to his daughter at birth was so fitting—Faith. For a lot of reasons, Faith was such a beautiful bride that day.

As you continue your reading through this devotional, I want to encourage you to focus on the Central Practices, for the more we live out our lives in Christ the more we build our hope in him. Hope isn't developed instantly; it takes time and consistency. As with any relationship, it is much easier to hope in someone when you know that they love you. Know that God loves you deeply. Hope in him.

PRAYER

Father, you are revealing the people and things in my life that I place too high of a hope in. I have trusted in them more than I have trusted in you. Please forgive me. Give me strength to surrender these things in this moment. And the next moment. And the one after that, that I may open myself to you and your love as I have not before. May my fears be overwhelmed by not just a hope, but a trust that you are good, and are worthy. Amen.

HUMILITY

I choose to esteem others above myself.

"Do nothing out of selfish ambition or vain conceit, but in humility consider others better than yourselves. Each of you should look not only to your own interests, but also to the interests of others."
Philippians 2:3-4

Jesus was the ultimate model of humility. He was born in a stable unfit for human birth. He responded to people with kindness and gracious mercy. Jesus countered culture with the message that whoever wanted to be great among others must be their servant. He even gave up his life for his enemies that they might experience the blessing of salvation. If any of us would desire to find a model of humility, we simply need to look at the Son of God.

Unfortunately, humility is not the natural disposition of man. Rather, humans seek to exalt themselves above all others. This self-idolatry is in all of us from the time we are born. The Bible tells us that "God opposes the proud but gives grace to the humble" (James 4:6). This verse reminds me that though I deserve his opposition, God chose to express generous, overflowing grace to me. He chose to save me, and in Christ to both humble me and make me humble.

As a redeemed child of God, I now have the power of Christ

to be humble before God and others. This is why Paul writes to the Christians in Philippi, "Do nothing out of selfish ambition or vain conceit. Rather, in humility value others above yourselves, not looking to your own interests but each of you to the interests of others" (Philippians 2:3-4). Pride is part of our old selves, and it must be rooted out by believers so they can experience shalom in their relationships with others. For a lack of humility is often in play when marriages break apart and churches split and friendships are broken.

Since humility is a distinguishing mark that helps us to shine the light of Christ in a world fueled by self-exaltation, let me suggest a few principles that will guide you in your pursuit of this significant virtue.

Humility and the Word

The goal of humility must begin with a right perspective of God, especially as it relates to the authority of his revealed Word. My pastor has led me to ask a critical question: "When I read Scripture, who will be King?" If the Bible says something that I disagree with, what do I do with that? Who wins in my thoughts about the issues of my day—what I believe or what Scripture says? Submitting to God's wisdom and ways is the first step in developing humility before others.

Humility and Prayer

How well do you listen when you pray? An article I read a few years ago shared that there is nothing more annoying than being in a conversation where the other person is dying to get all their words in, leaving you to feel like you are in a one-sided chat. Consider this concept when you pray. Do you sit in silence when you pray and allow the Lord to direct your heart and thoughts? Are you distracted by busyness, stress, or pain? Use

Scripture in your prayers to reorient yourself to a humble disposition, allowing the Lord to minister to your heart.

Humility and Worship

How much gratitude do you express in your worship? A worship leader once shared that the way you worship is evidence of the gratitude that you have in the Lord. When you assign all credit of goodness and blessing in your life to the Lord, then humble worship will flow from your heart. "Not to us, LORD, not to us but to your name be the glory" (Psalm 115:1). True humility leads to a contentment because you recognize that the Lord gives you all you need in life, and satisfaction will come when you finally stand before the Lord and are allowed entrance into the eternal kingdom.

PRAYER

Father, I desire nothing more than to honor you with my life. Help me to become more like Jesus every day by seeking to be humble. Give me humility to keep you King in my life each day. Help me to be humble as I engage with others in my home, my community, and the world around me. Thank you for your grace that saved me and the gift of the Holy Spirit that guides me and strengthens me to express the fruit of humility. To you, O Lord, be the glory and honor and praise. Amen.

JOY

I have inner contentment and purpose in spite of my circumstances.

"I have told you this so that my joy may be in you and that your joy may be complete."
John 15:11

"Running on fumes." This is the terrible realization that your fuel gauge is sitting on empty while you frantically scan the horizon for the nearest gas station. You've got nothing left in the tank and you hope you can make it to a refill.

Sometimes, we can feel like we're running on fumes in our life with God. Various things can drain our spiritual tank: trials, conflict, busyness, and sin. These things can deplete a person leaving them sad, hopeless, anxious, overwhelmed, and empty.

The opposite of this condition is joy. Joy is one of the fruits of the Holy Spirit—a virtue resulting from the Christian's momentary connection to God (Galatians 5:22). As we abide in Jesus, he produces joy in us. Unlike happiness, which is tied to our circumstances and can ebb and flow, joy is tied to Christ and is the condition of our heart when we remember that we are loved and are held securely in God's care. This is why a person can endure the most difficult circumstances and yet still possess radiant joy. They know who is in control.

Jesus prayed that his disciples' joy tank would be full (John 15:11). God calls all of creation to sing with joy (Psalm 65:8). However, joy isn't something that any person can manufacture. On cue, you can't just "be joyful." Joy is the byproduct of a person's pursuit of God. It's the glad reward of abiding.

The Bible highlights what we can do to discover greater joy. If your tank is empty, consider the following:

Behold the Beauty of God

The more you think about God—who he is and what he has done for you—the more your heart wells up with joy. In Psalm 4, the writer exclaims, "You have filled my heart with greater joy than when their grain and new wine abound" (v. 7). In other words, the harvest of my joy is overflowing. And the reason is because of the good things God has done; the light of his face has shined on his people (v. 6). Take a moment and think about God's forgiveness, his provision, his creativity, his faithfulness, his power, his blessings, his protection, his wisdom, and more. Take the attention off yourself and your circumstances and put it on God, and watch your joy abound. John Piper writes in *God Is the Gospel*, "In wonderful moments of illumination, there is a witness in our hearts: Soul-health and great joy come not from beholding a great self but a great splendor." As we behold the beauty of God, it's not difficult to "Rejoice in the Lord always" (Philippians 4:4).

Reflect on the Salvation of God

Frequently throughout the Bible, joy is linked to God's redeeming work. Rescue is always a reason for rejoicing! Isaiah writes, "I delight greatly in the LORD; my soul rejoices in my God. For he has clothed me with garments of salvation and arrayed me in a robe of righteousness" (Isaiah 61:10). So, take a moment to reflect. Your sin—past, present, and future—has been forgiven. Your guilt has been relieved. Your future is secure. You are saved and secure.

Steward the Life of God

A Golden Retriever is happiest when it's in the woods chasing squirrels, because it's doing what it was made to do. God's people are most glad when they are living out the life God designed for us. And what is the "good work" (Ephesians 2:10) God made you to do? Serve others. Share the gospel of Jesus. Give generously. Worship freely. Forgive graciously. Take a radical step of faith. All these things are joy-producers because they reflect a life lived in obedience to Christ. One writer said, "Joy is the flag which is flown from the castle of the heart when the King is in residence there."

PRAYER

Father, I beg you to increase my joy! My contentment is in you and not my circumstances. As I consider your beauty and the salvation you have given me in Christ, I invite joy to fill my heart. May your Holy Spirit empower me to live my new life in such a way that others are blessed, and I abound in spiritual joy. I am glad that you reside in the castle of my heart. Amen.

KINDNESS/GOODNESS

I choose to do the right things in my relationships with others.

"Make sure that nobody pays back wrong for wrong,
but always try to be kind to each other and everyone else."
1 Thessalonians 5:15

On Christmas Eve after circling a Target parking lot for what felt like hours, I happened upon the perfect parking spot right up front. I waited patiently with my blinker on while the car backed out of the space, but before I could pull in, another car snuck in and stole the spot. Are you kidding me? What was that?! The terrible injustice of it all left me slack-jawed and astounded at the world. Who in the world is mean enough to steal a parking spot on Christmas Eve? I wanted to hunt that shopper down and give him a piece of my mind, but thankfully I had 15 minutes of circling the parking lot to cool down.

Kindness and goodness should be an elementary steppingstone in the hierarchy of decent behavior. In fact, I'm pretty sure every elementary school has at least one special project to promote kindness: a board in the hallway with an endless supply of sticky notes to acknowledge others who have shown kindness, weekly random acts of kindness challenges, monthly awards for that one kid that nails it, and crafts and calendars that promote being bucket fillers, not bucket spillers. You'll find slogans on T-shirts, yard signs, animal shelters, and even decals for your favorite cup, saying, "Spread kindness like glitter!" or "Be a good human!"

We all want to live in a world filled with kind people where goodness overflows in abundance, but that seems to be the stuff of Hollywood. What's more, although it shouldn't be, kindness can be confusing. Cultural kindness is dramatically different from biblical kindness. Cultural kindness promotes tolerance but with an absence of love, kind of a "grit your teeth and bear it" outlook. A follower of Christ should show kindness not out of obligation or in the spirit of tolerance, but out of the overflow of love that Christ has shown us. Ephesians 4:32 encourages us to "Be kind and compassionate to one another, forgiving each other, just as in Christ God forgave you." Cultural kindness promotes goodness up to a certain point and then calls you foolish for allowing the boundary to be crossed, where biblical goodness endures for the long haul. Galatians 6:9 tells followers of Christ, "Let us not become weary in doing good, for at the proper time we will reap a harvest if we do not give up."

Kindness/Goodness is choosing to always do the right thing in our relationships with others, especially when we've been wronged. It's keeping short accounts and acting with an urgency to make things right during times of strife or hardship. Imagine being the first to recognize and admit your own mistakes and ask for forgiveness, the first to extend a helping hand, and the first to throw out a lifeline of human decency to your family, neighbors, and especially those on the margins. Kindness is a fruit of the Spirit (Galatians 5:22-23) that grows and spreads the closer our walk is to the Lord. If you're struggling in this area, ask God to soften your heart and remind you of the kindness he's shown to you. Prayerfully ask God to take those things that are roadblocks (anger, bitterness, indifference, or fear) and replace them with compassion and love for the people He created and loves.

PRAYER

Father, I confess I'm not as kind as I want to be. Remind me of the ways you've been faithful in my life and shown kindness to me. Cause me to recognize the goodness you've shown me and allow this to overflow in my heart, spilling over to others and pointing them to you. Amen.

LOVE

I sacrificially and unconditionally love and forgive others.

"This is love: not that we loved God, but that he loved us and sent his Son as an atoning sacrifice for our sins. Dear friends, since God so loved us, we also ought to love one another. No one has ever seen God; but if we love one another, God lives in us, and his love is made complete in us."
1 John 4:10-12

We love pizza. We love puppies. We love our kids. We love Jesus. The English word "love" needs some help, doesn't it? What's the difference between loving pizza and loving our kids? We love them both, but not in the same way. What would you do to show the extent of your love for a good deep dish Chicago style pizza? Now what would you do to show your love for your children? The gap between those two loves is pretty significant, I would hope.

I propose that the value one places on a person or thing determines the sacrifice of self that you would be willing to make for that object. Our chosen verse for the Central Virtue of Love (1 John 4:10-12) reveals the extent of God's love for us—he was willing to give fully of himself by sending his Son for us. Jesus, then, willingly bore our sin and the punishment it deserved. How great the love of the Father and the Son for us!

God did not send his Son to die for us because we loved him so much. In fact, just the opposite was true. "While we were still sinners, Christ died for us" (Romans 5:8). God loved us first and his love changed us from enemies to friends. We went from dead in our sins to alive in Christ. We went from hopeless and hell-bound to saved and sealed by the Holy Spirit.

So based on this amazing, unfailing, and unconditional love that God has for us, his children, we are called to sacrificially love and forgive others. To struggle with this is to somehow not fully comprehend and appreciate the depth of sacrificial love that God shown to us through Christ. However, we all struggle to love others this deeply. Thankfully, God invites us to consider the fact that Christ now "dwells in our hearts" and so his love can be expressed through us. Consider Paul's prayer in Ephesians 3:14-19:

"For this reason, I kneel before the Father, from whom every family in heaven and on earth derives its name. I pray that out of his glorious riches he may strengthen you with power through his Spirit in your inner being, so that Christ may dwell in your hearts through faith. And I pray that you, being rooted and established in love, may have power, together with all the Lord's holy people, to grasp how wide and long and high and deep is the love of Christ, and to know this love that surpasses knowledge—that you may be filled to the measure of all the fullness of God."

May we pray and ask the Holy Spirit to help us grasp and give away this love that "surpasses knowledge."

PRAYER

God, I want this to be true in my heart. I know it is your desire that I know your unfathomable love. You want me to experience it. Please strengthen me in my inner being so that Christ is at home in my heart and not just a visitor. As I experience your indescribable love, my love for others will overflow in my heart, in my words, and in my actions. I can love out of simple obedience, but you want me to love out of the abundant overflow of your love through me! I know that you can do this, and I ask that you would. In Jesus' name, Amen.

PATIENCE

I take a long time to overheat and endure patiently under the unavoidable pressures of life.

"A patient man has great understanding,
but a quick-tempered man displays folly."
Proverbs 14:29

It's not a secret in my family that I lack patience. I don't enjoy waiting; not for my toast in the morning or the shopper ahead of me in line. If you're like me, your feelings toward patience may include resistance and a bit of an eye roll. Patience requires us to endure through something hard, even if it's a small inconvenience. It feels good to have this validated in the very definition of the word:

Patience: To be of a long spirit, not to lose heart
- A. bravely enduring misfortunes and troubles
- B. bearing the offenses and injuries of others
    1. to be mild and slow in avenging
    2. to be long suffering, slow to anger, slow to punish

"Enduring...bearing...long suffering." This is the real burn of patience—the slow enduring of pain or unfairness without retaliation; not getting our way without getting heated. Our culture has made it even more difficult to be patient. Think same-day shipping, express checkout, 280 characters or less. We can usually get what we want. But we all need patience at some point, a little grace when we're struggling. When patience is offered it is comforting, disarming even. It's good news for someone in trouble. And isn't this how God's patience plays out in our own lives? As a display of God's patience toward us, he sent his Son who, for the joy set before him, endured the cross for our sin. "He is patient with you, not wanting anyone to perish, but everyone to come to repentance" (2 Peter 3:9). Christ let go of his right to comfort or personal justice, willingly bearing our offenses in his gruesome death. He suffered long. He humbly gave up a fight he could have won. This is true patience.

When God passed before Moses, he even included the virtue of patience in his own name, "The LORD, the LORD, the compassionate and gracious God, slow to anger, abounding in love and faithfulness..." (Exodus 34:6). Slow to anger. These are the exact words in the definition of patience. It is God's essence, God's own description of himself. This makes patience a key player in sharing God with the world. In patiently bearing offenses, we give others an encounter with the very character of God. "Warn those who are idle and disruptive, encourage the disheartened, help the weak, be patient with everyone" (1 Thessalonians 5:14). There are so many practical ways to do this! It makes patience a game in kindness and gospel action. By gladly waiting for a child to put on her shoes or a neighbor to mow his lawn, we play our hand. Even better, we can help the child tie the bow or lend a hand with the yard work.

Practice Your Patience Game

If you want to master patience, you must be intentional about addressing it in your life.

Try this:

1. Write down 3 circumstances in which you struggle to exhibit patience (e.g., traffic, in the doctor's waiting room, idling in line at the drive-thru).

2. Next to each, write a specific way you might exhibit patience. What would it look like practically in those situations? What could you call to mind? What would help you to be at peace and patient?

PRAYER

Patient Father, thank you for making provision for me when I was in trouble. Thank you, Christ, for suffering long for me. Teach me to see people in trouble and offer patience as a display of your character. Allow me to choose discomfort in these areas listed, to be slow to anger in the midst of discomfort or loss. Help me lay down my life for others as you laid down yours. Amen.

PEACE

I am free from anxiety because things are right between God, myself, and others.

"Do not be anxious about anything, but in everything, by prayer and petition, with thanksgiving, present your requests to God. And the peace of God, which transcends all understanding, will guard your hearts and your minds in Christ Jesus."
Philippians 4:6-7

In 1976, on their debut, self-titled album, Boston released the song "Peace of Mind." This anthemic song spoke to the multiple things that fill us with stress and anxiety and ultimately rob us of peace. One of the choruses declared, "all I want is to have my peace of mind." This wasn't just true in 1976; across generations and geographies people are looking to have consistent, long-lasting peace. But the questions have always been "How do we have peace?" and "How do we maintain our peace?"

When we come to Paul's words in Philippians 4:6-7, we can quickly dismiss them to the category of "easier said than done." However, if we probe a little deeper in this passage, we see that Paul does so much more than give us a trite suggestion for dealing with anxiety. For Paul, peace is not simply a fleeting feeling or distant desire but is rooted in intentionally giving our challenges over to Jesus and choosing to trust him.

The reality, experience, and enjoyment of peace is ultimately found in our understanding of God's sovereignty. If we truly believe that God is in control of all things in heaven and on earth, then we also need to believe that he is in control of our lives and circumstances. In times of anxiety, we can live in peace because we are in right standing with God, having received his Son as our Savior, and with others having no unresolved conflicts or problems, being peaceable so long as it depends on us.

When the Lord placed on my heart the desire for seminary, I was terrified! Not only was school incredibly difficult for me, but I was barely scraping by on the financial side of things. The more I prayed and sought clarity, the more I knew that God was calling me to trust him with my education, my finances, and my living situation. By the grace of God, I was able to complete seminary in three years without accruing any further financial debt, and I always had all of my needs covered. Through surrendering to God's plan and trusting that he is always good, I learned to trust him more deeply and have persevering peace in the midst of uncertainty.

PRAYER

Father, you are good. Thank you for the fact that you are never caught off guard by circumstances or situations. Thank you that you are sovereign. In the midst of anxiousness, I ask that you constantly bring to mind Paul's words of prayer and surrender and remind me of your peace that transcends all understanding. Thank you for sending your Son and allowing me, by your grace, to be in right standing with you. Amen.

SELF-CONTROL

I have the power, through Christ, to control myself.

"For the grace of God that brings salvation has appeared to all men.
It teaches us to say 'No' to ungodliness and worldly passions, and to
live self-controlled, upright and godly lives in this present age,
while we wait for the blessed hope—the glorious appearing
of our great God and Savior, Jesus Christ."
Titus 2:11-13

Self-control is listed as one of the fruits of the Spirit in Galatians 5, but its name may lead you to wrongly conclude that it is ultimately up to you to control yourself. After all, it is self-control. However, the root meaning of self-control is a mastery of self that proceeds from within oneself, not by oneself. Therefore, self-control is actually less about our ability to control ourselves and far more about our ability to surrender to God's Spirit within us. Romans 8:7-9 says, "For the mind that is set on the flesh is hostile to God, for it does not submit to God's law; indeed, it cannot. Those who are in the flesh cannot please God. You, however, are not in the flesh but in the Spirit, if in fact the Spirit of God dwells in you." But you are not entirely off the hook. We who walk in the Spirit now have the power to say "no" to worldly passions, but it is not always easy to do. At any moment we can live for ourselves and bring forth the marks of the flesh, or we can submit to the Spirit and harvest the fruit of self-control from within.

Here are four ways you can partner with the Spirit to accomplish self-control:

Prepare the Soil

Cultivating the soil is a vital process in farming that breaks through the crusty surface in order to uproot weeds and make room for new roots. You can prepare your heart to receive the seed of self-control by first confessing your lack of it and asking God to forgive you and enable you to surrender to his Spirit and say no to your flesh.

James 4:2—"You do not have, because you do not ask."

Root Your Affections in Jesus

Once the weeds of the flesh have been uprooted, your heart can begin to take root in the love of Christ who died so that you might no longer live for yourself but for him.

2 Corinthians 5:14-15—"For the love of Christ controls us, because we have concluded this: that one has died for all, therefore all have died; and he died for all, that those who live might no longer live for themselves but for him who for their sake died and was raised."

Plant Your Mind on God's Will

The weeds of fleshly living have been uprooted by confession and repentance, and the roots of Christ's love have settled deep into your heart. Now you must decide in your mind that you will stay planted where you are when the storms of life try to uproot you.

1 Peter 4:1-2—"Since therefore Christ suffered in the flesh, arm yourselves with the same way of thinking, for whoever has suffered in the flesh has ceased from sin, so as to live for the rest of the time in the flesh no longer for human passions but for the will of God."

Protect the Harvest

As the harvest of self-control begins to flourish, be prepared to protect your crop from enemies that seek to devour it.

1 Peter 5:8—"Be sober-minded; be watchful. Your adversary the devil prowls around like a roaring lion, seeking someone to devour."

PRAYER

Father, I confess I have been living for myself. Forgive me for my selfish ways. Cultivate in me a deeper love for you and your kingdom than for me and mine. Help me, Lord, to be deeply rooted in the love of Christ and to remain in your will through the storms of this life and the enemy's attacks. I pray that you would be glorified through the harvest of self-control that your Spirit will produce from within. Amen.

CENTRAL PRACTICES

BIBLE STUDY

I study the Bible to know God, the truth, and to find direction for my daily life.

"For the word of God is living and active. Sharper than any double-edged sword, it penetrates even to dividing soul and spirit, joints and marrow; it judges the thoughts and attitudes of the heart."
Hebrews 4:12

The Bible is the most unique and powerful book in the entire world because it is the inspired Word of God. It is the only tangible resource we have that conveys God's power to save, sanctify, and equip its readers to serve him and others. As disciples (i.e., learners) of Jesus, it is important for us to learn to study the Bible, not simply read or hear it.

Studying the Bible is part of God's plan to carry out his purposes in the lives of believers. In fact, Paul explained to Timothy that God had used his Word in Timothy's life for his salvation, sanctification, and service. Look at what the Apostle wrote in 2 Timothy 3:15-17: "and how from infancy you have known the Holy Scriptures, which are able to make you wise for salvation through faith in Christ Jesus. All Scripture is God-breathed and is useful for teaching, rebuking, correcting, and training in righteousness, so that the servant of God may be thoroughly equipped for every good work."

For Bible study to be transformational in our lives, we need to have a faithful process that helps us arrive at the correct interpretation and application. One method that has been used by many is called *inductive Bible study*. Consider the following process:

Observation

This essential first step in Bible study is to ask the question, "What do I see in the text?" Who is the author? To whom is he writing? What is the author's primary reason for writing the book? When and where was it written? What is the historical and cultural context of this time and region? Read over the passages again. Note repetitive words and ideas, changes in theme or time, contrasts, cause and effect. Look for any and all details that the Lord may show you.

Interpretation

This second step asks the question, "What does it mean?" The goal here is to discover the primary meaning that the author originally intended. What is the author's point? What prompted the author to write? What sin is being addressed? What truth or exhortation is being given? What other Scripture might help to better interpret this passage? Ask yourself if you have overlooked anything or made any assumptions. Once you have exhausted these questions, you are better prepared to identify the author's main point.

Application

The final step of Bible study answers the question, "How does it work?" How is God calling me to apply this passage to my life? The most important part of Bible study is not what you learn from it but rather what you do with it. After all, it is meant to produce good works. Consider what the Bible says in James

1:25, "But whoever looks intently into the perfect law that gives freedom, and continues in it—not forgetting what they have heard, but doing it—they will be blessed in what they do." In order to accurately understand how God wants you to apply a specific scripture to your life, it is crucial that you spend time with him in prayer. The possibilities are endless. He may be making you aware of sin in your life, reminding you of a foundational truth, or preparing you for where he is leading you next.

PRAYER

Father, thank you for the gift of the Bible. Without it I shudder to think where I would be today. Through the power of your Word, you have saved me, and are faithfully sanctifying and equipping me for your service. Your Word is a lamp to my feet and light to my path (Psalm 119:105). Help me to treasure it. I pray, Father, that you would fill me with a deep longing to spend time with you in your Word and give me the wisdom required to interpret and apply your powerful words to my life. In Jesus' name, Amen.

BIBLICAL COMMUNITY

I fellowship with other Christians to accomplish God's purposes in my life, others' lives, and in the world.

"All the believers were together and had everything in common. Selling their possessions and goods, they gave to anyone as he had need. Every day they continued to meet together in the temple courts. They broke bread in their homes and ate together with glad and sincere hearts, praising God and enjoying the favor of all the people. And the Lord added to their number daily those who were being saved."
Acts 2:44-47

God created us to carry out life with other people. His Church is a perfect expression of this reality. Though we are each individual members of Christ's Body, we are not whole unless we are integrated with the other parts. Beyond these theological truths, we also find that Christians flourish when they are part of a small group of committed believers who are intentional in their spiritual formation together. This is what we call Biblical Community.

In Acts 2:44-47 we see the early Church providing us a model of what Biblical Community can be:

"All the BELIEVERS"

Now, this is not to say that you cannot invite your unbelieving friend to join you for your weekly community gatherings. However, it is important to note that as you journey through all of life's ups and downs together, you are going to want other brothers and sisters in Christ, who hold fast to God's Word as authority, to lean on.

"were TOGETHER"

This is a pretty obvious one—you have to meet together to have Biblical Community. Unfortunately, too many times, people become distracted with the busyness of life, and they place Biblical Community on the back burner. It is important to find a group of people who recognize that life can get busy, but that will fight for regular time together (Hebrews 10:25). I've always known this to be true: You make time for the people who are important to you.

"everything in COMMON"

People are naturally drawn to others who are in similar stages of life or have similar interests. But the key thing to have in common with others in Biblical Community is the love of Christ and a heart for the gospel to saturate every area of life. This is why diversity in Biblical Community can be so healthy—we keep the main thing the main thing and look to learn from others who may have a different experience from our own.

"selling/giving to anyone in NEED"

One of the greatest joys of being a part of a Biblical Community is when you get to bless or are blessed by the generosity of others in your group. To know that needs can be brought to your community from within provides amazing opportunities for generosity to be expressed.

"They BROKE BREAD...with glad/sincere hearts"

Think back on your life. So many times when great things have happened, food was probably involved. Eat together. Be nourished together.

"PRAISING God"

Now it's not much of a Biblical Community if you never spend time growing closer to God. Center your time together around approaching his throne in prayer. Open his Word together. Serve together. As you do, God will use the members of your group to strengthen one another (Proverbs 27:17) and cause you reflect his image more and more.

The importance of Biblical Community cannot be emphasized enough. Believers were not created to go through this life alone. Search hard for community. When you find it, fight for it. Give of yourself and watch the Lord bless your understanding of what it means to dwell in unity (Psalm 133:1).

PRAYER

Father, thank you so much for providing me with others to journey alongside in this life. Help me to never take this gift for granted. Spur me on to ways to bless those around me. Use me to draw others closer to you. We want to be a light in our community that reflects your glory day to day. Amen.

COMPASSION

I seek to serve the last, the least, and the lost in my community.

"Defend the weak and the fatherless; uphold the cause of the poor and the oppressed. Rescue the weak and the needy; deliver them from the hand of the wicked."
Psalm 82:3-4

Do you consider yourself to be a compassionate person? This question is one of many that would land on a self-assessment for those who seek to be on the growth path to be more like Jesus. Compassion is an important practice of the Christian life. Compassion International, a Christian organization seeking to care for children around the world who live in significant poverty, offers a compelling definition of compassion. They believe that having compassion is recognizing the suffering of others and then taking action to help. The Latin root word for compassion is *pati,* which means "to suffer," and the prefix *com* means "with." *Compassion* literally means "to suffer with."

The challenge for most of us is twofold. First, we struggle to be aware that someone is suffering. Often, we are not personally connected to people deeply enough to know if they are suffering or the ways in which they suffer. Secondly, we are at a loss of what to do when we know someone is suffering. Often our quick fix efforts can end up hurting more than helping.

Let me offer some advice to address these challenges.

Recognize the Need

One in five adults in the United States experienced mental illness over the past year. This is a consistent and staggering statistic indicating the level at which people are suffering. This fact only highlights the mental suffering. There are many who suffer physically, emotionally, spiritually, and relationally as well. Stop and observe those around you each day. Discard the devices of our day and engage more deeply with those closest to you. Chances are, someone in your home is suffering.

Make a list of the top 10 people you are closest to in your life, not just family, and commit to communicating with them more often than you have in the past. Be intentional to set aside time to chat about life and focus on the blessings and the challenges each person faces. What questions could you ask someone that would help you know them better and understand their needs? Once you recognize the needs, you might just be able to bring some peace in your response.

Respond with Compassion

Paul writes that Christians should rejoice with those who rejoice and mourn with those who mourn (Romans 12:15). Both actions require engagement with others at a deep level. Rejoicing with and mourning with suggest that compassionate people come alongside others in times of celebration and in times of great trials. They are not afraid to get dirty when suffering is taking place, to help with wise counsel, or to serve when a practical need has come up. This kind of compassion builds stronger bonds and unifies the body of Christ.

People might experience compassion from you if you sit and listen to their hurts and pray with them in a season of worry or pain. They might feel your compassion if you were to help them with practical needs such as mowing their lawn or cleaning their home when they are experiencing significant physical pain. Compassion on display communicates the love that God desires from his people.

Jesus modeled for his disciples what it meant to be compassionate. He fed the hungry, healed the sick, exorcised demons, listened to people as they came to share their hurts, and brought overwhelming peace. The disciples stood by, watching and serving Jesus as he worked. Jesus charged his disciples to go into the world to recognize the needs of all people and to respond with compassion. In compassion they shared the good news of the gospel, cast out evil spirits, and healed sickness just as Christ had done. This work was not possible without the power, authority, and capacity for compassion given only by the almighty God, through the work of the Son, and by the power of the Holy Spirit. Jesus commissions us to continue his work of compassion (John 20:21), and makes his transforming power available to all who believe and seek to carry out his will (John 14:12-13).

PRAYER

Father, compassion is not an easy practice, yet you call me to be compassionate to all people. Thank you for your Word that explicitly tells me what it means to be compassionate. Thank you for the ministry of Jesus whose beautiful compassion is on display. Help me to recognize when people are in need, and help me to respond with appropriate and loving compassion to be an instrument of peace in other people's lives. Whether it is by word or deed, may the gospel go forth to those who are suffering. Amen.

DISCIPLE-MAKING

I multiply godly beliefs, virtues and practices in others to encourage their spiritual growth in Christ.

"And the things you have heard me say in the presence of many witnesses entrust to reliable people who will also be qualified to teach others."
2 Timothy 2:2

I didn't attend church when I was a child. In fact, my family never really talked about God, Jesus, or religion. The most I knew about the Creator of the world is that my grandma sang weird songs with "thou" and "thee" while she was cleaning. Fast forward some years, and at the age of 26, I gave my life to God and asked Jesus to be my Savior. I knew nothing. Zero. Thankfully, I had a wonderful friend who invested in me and dropped nuggets of truth into my lap for years. She was an amazing disciple and I remember wondering, "Why is she helping me? Am I really worth it?"

What compels a person to disciple another? What moves their heart and causes them to pour themselves out, investing so deeply in another? Jesus' parting words to the Eleven in Matthew 28:19-20, "Therefore go and make disciples of all nations, baptizing them in the name of the Father and of the Son and of the Holy Spirit, and teaching them to obey everything I have commanded you." What did my friend do to disciple me?

What does it take to be a disciple maker?

Time

A disciple maker makes sacrifices to spread the good news (Hebrews 13:16). My friend spent time with me despite having newborn twins and a husband who had not yet trusted Christ. She very easily could have passed me to someone else or said she was too busy, but she shared her most precious resource with me, her time.

Patience

When I spouted out worldly and grossly incorrect opinions about my off-kilter theology, she never told me I was wrong (it's almost embarrassing to look back and see just how wrong I was). With "great patience and careful instruction" (2 Timothy 4:2), she asked lots of questions, opened God's Word, and directed me to Jesus.

Love

She clearly followed the commands in Mark 12:30-31 to love God and love your neighbor. Her love for God's Word was an inspiration to me. She knew so much! She loved me. As broken, wrong, and misguided as I was, she loved me enough to invest herself in my spiritual growth. She even gifted me a Bible that her dad had given to her until I could get one of my own. The outpouring of this love brings me to tears still today.

Single-Mindedness

A disciple maker is one who seeks God's kingdom and righteousness first (Matthew 6:33). I imagine it must have been difficult for my mentor to put up with my stubborn ways and resistance to change. She was persistent, gracious, steadfast, and always loving in her approach. Her goal was not to see me be a better human, it was to help me develop into a follower of Christ, a disciple myself.

Believers are called to disciple, to intentionally help other believers grow in Christ and multiple godly beliefs, virtues, and practices in others. Your godly wisdom is a gift to be shared. Be it in the home or at work or with a friend, you have something to offer.

PRAYER

Heavenly Father, help me to love you so much that the outpouring of this love flows to other people. Help me see others the way that you do and be willing to give my time and energy investing in their spiritual growth. Give me a desire to show others your love and help them grow closer to you. Amen.

EVANGELISM

I share Jesus with others through personal proclamation and demonstration of the gospel.

"But you will receive power when the Holy Spirit comes on you; and you will be my witnesses in Jerusalem, and in all Judea and Samaria, and to the ends of the earth."
Acts 1:8

Every week we go to the University of Texas at Arlington campus to share the gospel with college students. I remember one day when we walked up, there was a man standing on a rock and holding a sign. The sign read, "Ask me why God says you're going to hell!" As you might have guessed there was an angry mob of students around this guy shouting objections, hurling insults, and spewing all types of profanity. Even the cops were called to keep peace! All the while this man kept preaching the gospel and shouting above the crowd's objections. The Bible does say that we must have faith in Christ for our salvation, and anyone who does not believe will spend an eternity apart from God. So, the message was correct, but his method was driving a wedge between him and his audience.

We often focus on the verses and the methods for sharing the gospel, but we often forget to prepare the path for the gospel to be heard. It has become a guiding principle for me to remember that Christ came full of grace and truth. Both of these are important and should be held in balance. We tend to favor one or the other. Sometimes we are very gracious and so much so that we compromise on the truth of God. Other times, we hammer away at the truth and forget to be gracious to those who need that truth. Jesus figured out the balance and he was full of grace and truth. The result was a compelling and refreshing life that continues to inspire believers and non-believers.

The truth of the gospel is found all throughout the Bible. Romans 6:23 says, "the wages of sin is death, but the gift of God is eternal life in Christ Jesus our Lord." Romans 10:9 explains how to receive that gift: "If you declare with your mouth, 'Jesus is Lord,' and believe in your heart that God raised him from the dead, you will be saved." These statements sum the gospel up well.

The greatness and free availability of God's gift, along with the eternal consequences of not receiving it, should compel us to share the gospel with anyone we can. We have the hope the world needs, and without Christ, they have no way of getting it. With him, they have hope not only for eternity but also for today. And he's given us the privilege and responsibility to introduce them to him (Matthew 28:18-20; 2 Corinthians 5:18-19).

Therefore, the truth of the gospel needs to be firmly within our grasp. I encourage you to familiarize yourself with two or three methods for sharing the gospel (and there are many to choose from), and to look for opportunities to bring it to bear in your conversations and interactions with others.

But just as firmly as we hold to the truth of the gospel, we need to be devoted to a gracious approach. More often than not, people will disagree with us when we share the gospel. I have often found myself in a debate that could have easily turned into a shouting match. Disagreement often can spin out of control, but a gracious answer dissipates even the quickest tempers.

God is ultimately the one who changes hearts. Neither our words nor our gracious actions can change someone, but God employs our words and our actions to draw the listener closer to him. The love that we show truly reflects the love of God, and people get a glimpse of what the Lord has to offer to all who believe.

When we display God's love and hope in our lives, people may be curious about its source. First Peter 3:15 tells us, "Always be prepared to give an answer to everyone who asks you to give the reason for the hope that you have," but also reminds us to "do this with gentleness and respect."

Being right rarely draws people to Christ, but showing God's love does.

PRAYER

Dear Father, would you help me to communicate the truth of the gospel to anyone who crosses my path? Give me boldness to speak up, even when it's unpopular to do so. Please help me see people as you see them and to show them your love. Help me to prepare the path for the gospel by living full of grace and truth. I pray you empower me to be your witness wherever you put me. Amen.

GENEROSITY

I gladly give my resources to fulfill God's purposes.

"You will be enriched in every way so that you can be generous
on every occasion, and through us your generosity
will result in thanksgiving to God."
2 Corinthians 9:11

The Mazatec Indians of southwestern Mexico believe that there is only so much good, so much knowledge, or so much love to go around. So, a craftsman doesn't teach his trade because he's afraid he'll lose some of his skill. Parents are hesitant to have a second child out of fear of having to divide their limited love between two children. To say "Have a good day" is to give away some of your happiness.

The greatest challenge to generous living is that some people believe that they'll have less if they give more away. However, the Bible teaches just the opposite.

One of the reasons that the Apostle Paul wrote his second letter to the Corinthians was to prepare the church for a collection that he would be requesting to help the Christians in Jerusalem who had fallen on hard times. Regarding their contribution, Paul emphasized that, though giving is a matter of personal conviction (9:7), God intends every Christian to practice charity. He names several reasons why generosity is so important.

First, generosity is a "good work" reflective of God at work in our lives (v. 8). In Ephesians 2:10, Paul wrote that Christians are "created in Christ Jesus to do good works, which God prepared in advance for us to do." God intends to make his grace and kindness known in the world and these virtues often show themselves through the generosity of his people. When we give, we are reflecting our new nature as God's people, and we join God in his plan to bless the world.

Second, our generosity will lead to gladness in God among others. As our giving overflows into the lives of our neighbors, their hearts will overflow in thanksgiving to God (vv. 11-12). Recipients of our kindness will be led to think about the One who provides "every good and perfect gift" (James 1:17). In this way, every generous gesture is a like a signpost pointing to heaven. When you give, you communicate that God is good, more than you are.

Third, our generosity cultivates more for us to give away. As we give our time, our talents, or our treasure, God will "supply and increase your store of seed and will enlarge the harvest of your righteousness" (v. 10). The more you give, the more God gives for you to give away. Paul states it plainly in v. 6: "Whoever sows sparingly will also reap sparingly, and whoever sows generously will also reap generously."

So, generosity benefits us, others, and the glory of God. But what is true generosity? If a man has $100 and gives away $1, is this a generous gift? How about $20 or $90? Or is the woman who lets her neighbor borrow her car more generous than the one who gives her neighbor a cup of flour? How can we measure true generosity?

The standard that applies no matter the size of a person's resource or gift is the standard of faith. When we give an amount that requires us to trust God, that amount fits the definition of generosity. A single mother who can barely make ends meet is likely more generous when she gives $10 to help a friend than the couple who makes $150,000 and can give $500 without even thinking about it. God is not as concerned with the amount of the gift as he is the amount of faith required to give it. This is why Jesus commended the widow who gave two mites. It was not the amount of her offering but the extent of her sacrifice that mattered. Trust God in your giving and you will be truly generous. And, by being truly generous, you will lose nothing and gain everything in return.

PRAYER

Father, I thank you for your generosity in giving your Son to me. How extravagant is the gift of salvation! Lead me to greater faith as I express increasing generosity to people around me. I want to join you in your redemptive work and lead others to look to you as I express your grace through my giving. I believe that the more I give away, the more blessing I will experience from you. Amen.

PRAYER

I pray to God to know him, to lay my request before him and to find direction for my daily life.

"Come and listen, all you who fear God; let me tell you what he has done for me. I cried out to him with my mouth; his praise was on my tongue. If I had cherished sin in my heart, the Lord would not have listened; but God has surely listened and heard my voice in prayer. Praise be to God, who has not rejected my prayer or withheld his love from me!"
Psalm 66:16-20

Relationship Lesson 101: We talk to people to build a relationship with them. You can choose a variety of mediums of communication, but whatever way you choose, the more time you spend and talking you do with that person, the better you know them, right? The closer you become.

This is true with us and God, as well. Time spent in conversation with God leads to a closer relationship with him. The religious word for talking with God is "prayer," but that word can be a hurdle for many people to face. It can create a sense of nervousness and intimidation, a concern about doing it wrong. The whole "Holy of Holies" thing in the Old Testament supports the idea that entering into the presence of God Almighty should be done with a good dose of fear and trembling. But when Jesus died for our sins on the cross 2,000 years ago, the literal Holy of Holies curtain in the temple was torn in two (from top to bottom). That communicated a clear statement to the world that the door to the throne of grace was now open wide through Christ.

Jesus covered our sins by his shed blood, and by grace through faith in him, we have been washed clean, forgiven, and now, as children of God, we can come boldly before him. No fear or trembling required. So, what do we do now? How do we pray?

When we need something, we ask for it. When we feel grateful, we say "Thank You" to the Lord. When we are amazed at His goodness and greatness, we brag to God about God. When we're not sure what we're supposed to do, we ask him for help. When we mess up and we know it, we admit it and thank him for his forgiveness. Requests, thanksgiving, praises, adoration, petitions, and forgiveness. It's like a real relationship with a person because it is a real relationship with a Person. Talking and listening. Growing in our relationship with God through prayer.

May I add one more perspective in this discussion about talking with God? As hard as it might be to actually believe, God yearns for us to talk with him. Not that he needs anything from us; the truth is that he knows we need everything from him. He has everything we need. He is everything we need. And he will remind us in not-so-subtle ways of our critical dependence on him. Pain and exhaustion are great teachers. Desperation and dryness alert our awareness of need. In Psalm 63:1, David gasps a prayer when his body and soul are dry and weary. "You, God, are my God, earnestly I seek you; I thirst for you, my whole being longs for you, in a dry and parched land where there is no water." David did not lift up a casual call to the Lord. He didn't wait his turn or apologize for interrupting. David was at the end of his rope. He was distressed and disturbed and he passionately prayed to his God. That was his pattern.

In Luke 18, Jesus teaches us that we should always pray with persistence, even impatience, to our Heavenly Father. He tells a parable about a needy widow bugging her neighbor, the local judge, demanding that he give her justice against her adversary.

She wouldn't leave him alone until she got him to respond, and he finally did because of her "nagging." She wouldn't wait till the morning, leave a message, or be dissuaded. Jesus commended this kind of praying. How much more does our gracious and generous Father in heaven love to hear his children crying out to him, believing that he is the source of relief and rescue that they are so desperate for.

Listen to God's urging of his people to call to him in prayer with determination:

"Seek the Lord and his strength; seek his presence continually!" (1 Chronicles 16:11)

"You will seek me and find me, when you seek me with all your heart." (Jeremiah 29:13)

"Continue steadfastly in prayer, being watchful in it with thanksgiving." (Colossians 4:2)

"Let us then approach God's throne of grace with confidence, so that we may receive mercy and find grace to help us in our time of need." (Hebrews 4:16)

So, let's talk to the Lord. Every day, anytime, about anything and everything. Don't wait. Don't let anything get in the way. We are thirsty. He offers us Living Water. We are hungry. He is the Bread of Life. We are sheep and he is our Shepherd, guiding and providing, protecting and correcting, filling us and forgiving us. Whenever we call, he will answer!

PRAYER

Today, make the prayer your own.

Father, …

SINGLE-MINDEDNESS

I focus on God and his priorities for my life.

"But seek first his kingdom and his righteousness,
and all these things will be given to you as well."
Matthew 6:33

I still remember when Kelly and I began dating, and I started to believe she was "the one." There was nothing else I could think about! My mind was transfixed upon her and our future together. All I wanted to do was spend time with her and get to know her better. Maybe you can remember a time like this when your whole world was singularly focused in one direction, for one purpose. It might have been when you were preparing to go to college or getting your home ready for your first baby. When we center our thoughts and attention on something to this degree, we're said to be single-minded.

At CBC we define single-mindedness in the Christian's life as being "focused on God and his priorities for my life." This means that the primary orientation of my life is meant to be bent toward the purposes of God. For this to be possible I need to do two things. First, I need to understand from God's Word what his desire is for my life. Second, I need to be willing to submit to God's purposes and plan for me.

Understanding God's Priorities

The Sermon on the Mount is the greatest sermon ever taught. In it, Jesus reveals his desire for his followers. In the high point of his sermon, Jesus calls upon us to "seek first his kingdom and his righteousness" (Matthew 6:33). The kingdom of God is his reign in and through his people. At present, the kingdom is manifest on earth through Spirit-filled followers of Christ who serve as ambassadors of his reign through the gospel. To seek "first" his kingdom and righteousness is to direct our energies towards the purpose of extending the reign of God's grace into the lives of others.

Seeking God's kingdom is a rich and integrated occupation. We do this by carrying out our daily work in a way that honors the Lord (Colossians 3:23), by teaching our children to know and obey God's Word (Ephesians 6:4), by showing kindness to neighbors and strangers (Mark 12:31), by opening our mouths with truth that can transform (2 Corinthians 6:7), by standing as advocates for the vulnerable (Proverbs 31:8-9), by sharing what we have with others (1 Timothy 6:17-19), and by setting our gaze on Jesus (Hebrews 12:2). Jonathan Edwards once wrote, "The seeking of the kingdom of God is the chief business of the Christian life."

Submitting to God's Priorities

Now that we have a better understanding of God's priorities for our lives, the question now is, "Are we willing to adjust our lives toward those purposes?" This is where the rubber meets the road. This is where faith is called to be put into action. Let me encourage you to ask several questions that might help you to have greater single-mindedness toward God and his priorities for your life:

After I die, when I stand before God, what will I have wanted my life to be most focused upon?

How am I presently seeking first God's kingdom and his righteousness?

What areas of my life—job, family, time, money—need the most redirection for me to be faithful to God's purposes and plan for me?

PRAYER

Father, I truly want to have my mind, my heart, and my life to be set upon you. However, I need your help. I so easily get distracted by things that aren't really that significant. I pray you would give me determination to be devoted first to you and your desire for people around me to know who Jesus is. May my single-mindedness to your kingdom purposes lead others to know you and worship you. Amen.

SPIRITUAL GIFTS

I know and use my spiritual gifts to accomplish God's purposes.

"Just as each of us has one body with many members, and these members do not all have the same function, so in Christ we who are many form one body, and each member belongs to all the others. We have different gifts, according to the grace given us."
Romans 12:4-6

What is your favorite hero movie? My favorites are the ones where an unknown, even unsuspected, "minor" character ends up being the one with the unique special gift which turns out to be one thing needed to save the day. Perhaps Samwise from The Lord of the Rings trilogy is one of these characters. As the best friend of Frodo (who saved all of Middle Earth by destroying the ring in Mordor), Samwise didn't have any particular strengths or possess any powerful weapons. Yet without his fierce dedication and constant encouragement, enemies would have prevailed. Frodo, the obvious hero, would not have triumphed if not for Samwise.

Whether you feel more like a Frodo (with obvious hero qualities) or more like Samwise (kind of ordinary or regular) in the practices of following Jesus, we each have a calling. No matter what you've done or where you've been, God has some ideas for you. And not only that, he has fashioned you in such a unique way. One of the primary ways God has done this is by giving you at least one spiritual gift. 1 Corinthians 12 states, "There are different kinds of spiritual gifts, but the same Spirit is the source of them all… A spiritual gift is given to each of us so we can help each other."

What Are the Gifts?

There are a few biblical texts that offer lists of spiritual gifts. First Corinthians 12 is a great beginning place. Among others, it includes the gifts of being apostles, teachers, prophets, helpers, and organizers. Another listing in Romans 12 includes: faith, serving, encouragement, generosity, leadership, and kindness. This isn't an exhaustive list. Take some time to do biblical digging and study.

How Do I Discover My Spiritual Gift?

That's a great question. Every Christ-follower should have a good sense of what their spiritual gift is. You can Google "spiritual gifts test." You'll find several that are free and reliable. Take one or two. You can also explore your giftings and fit in the context of a group setting. Exploring and sharing these discoveries in the context of a trusting and helpful small group will bring you great encouragement, affirmation, and accountability.

Why Has God Given Me a Spiritual Gift?

The Church, made up Christ-followers both local and global, is described in Scripture as a body. "The human body has many parts, but the many parts make up one whole body. So it is with the body of Christ… All of you together are Christ's body, and each of you is a part of it" (1 Corinthians 12). You are a unique part of this body of Christ. No one can do what you are designed to do in the body. So you have a purpose and a calling in God's work in the world and your spiritual gift is a part of your equipping. First Peter 4 states we "manage them (our gifts) well so that God's generosity can flow through you." It's worth noting that God is the one who determines which gift(s) you receive. You do not pick your spiritual gift. But what you'll find is that your giftings are custom fitted to you.

PRAYER

Father, I thank you that you call me your son/daughter. You have adopted me and I belong to you. And not only that, you have given me a place in your plans. You have ideas for me. Even though you didn't need me, you have included me. Thank you for such a precious love. Help me to discover the unique ways that you have gifted me. May I spend myself for your glory. As 1 Peter 4:11 says, may I "do it will all the strength and energy God supplies. Then everything [I] do will bring glory to God through Jesus Christ. All glory and power to him forever and ever. Amen."

WORSHIP

I worship God for who he is and what he has done for me.

"Come, let us sing for joy to the LORD; let us shout aloud to the Rock of our salvation. Let us come before him with thanksgiving and extol him with music and song. For the LORD is the great God, the great King above all gods. In his hand are the depths of the earth, and the mountain peaks belong to him. The sea is his, for he made it, and his hands formed the dry land. Come, let us bow down in worship, let us kneel before the LORD our Maker; for he is our God and we are the people of his pasture, the flock under his care."
Psalm 95:1-7

When we talk in church about worship, we often mean songs that we sing on Sunday morning. If we think the music is particularly good, we say things like, "I love my church; they have really great worship." Interestingly, the most common words used for worship in the Old and New Testaments don't actually mention music at all. The most common word translated to worship in the Old Testament is *shachah* which means "to bow down, prostrate oneself, before a monarch or superior, in homage." The most common Greek word used in the New Testament is *proskyneo* which means "to kiss the hand to (towards) one."

In ancient cultures it was common for people to bow face down in the presence of royalty as a gesture of deep reverence and humility. This would convey that the person bowing recognized their lowly status in the presence of a king and that they were in complete submission. So, what does it look like for a believer to worship God today?

Consider the following three aspects of worship and think about how they apply to your life:

Worship Is Personal

Paul tells us to offer our bodies as "living sacrifices" and calls it "true and proper worship" (Romans 12:1). If our whole bodies are meant to be a living sacrifice to the Lord, then it would imply that we have an opportunity to worship God in everything we do. When we choose to spend an evening serving at a food pantry instead of going out for dinner, that's worship. When we decide to forego buying as many Christmas gifts as possible for ourselves and family because we want to sponsor a family in need, that's worship. When we elect to prioritize things that spread the gospel, we worship.

Worship Is Congregational

There is something special that happens when the body of believers come together with the intention of celebrating God. The upward benefits are that we honor God and are reminded of his goodness to us, but there are lateral benefits as well. Paul encourages us to "spur one another on toward love and good deeds" (Hebrews 10:24-45). When we assemble on Sundays to sing songs together, observe communion together or study Scripture together, we get to worship God as well as serve each other in the process.

Worship Is Sacrificial

It's easy to give away something that's free. If I win tickets to a concert that I don't want to see, I'm not bothered if I give them to someone else. However, when we have to give up something we desire for someone else's sake, it can be more difficult. In 2 Samuel, King David refuses to build an altar with materials and animals that were offered to him for free. Why? In his words, "I will not sacrifice to the LORD my God burnt offerings that cost me nothing" (2 Samuel 24:24). Earnest worship, by its nature, requires that we sacrifice. That includes our time, our money, and our comforts, and for some it has meant their very lives.

PRAYER

Father, help me cultivate a spirit of sacrificial worship. Help me to see that there are chances to honor you even in mundane daily activities by giving myself away. Remind me often that when I experience the pain of sacrifice that Jesus first endured great suffering for my sake. May my worship of you in the stillness of solitude and in the great assembly be sweet incense set before you. I offer my actions, my resources, and my devotion wholly to you, oh God. Amen.

Contributors

The following ministry staff serve at Central Bible Church and have contributed to this work. We are grateful for the way they use their gifts for God's glory and are ever-growing in the Core Competencies of the spiritual life.

Nathan Beltran, *Worship Director*
Jenny Black, *Women's Minister*
Tom Bulick, *Spiritual Formation and Community Pastor*
David Daniels, *Lead Pastor*
Alison Dellenbaugh, *Spiritual Formation Resource Coordinator*
Manny Fernandez, *Student Pastor*
Brett Hansen, *Community Pastor*
Ryan Rasberry, *Community Pastor*
Jon Rhiddlehoover, *Lead Community Pastor*
Roger Sappington, *Executive Pastor*
Libby Slaughter, *Communications Director*
Stephanie Thomas, *Children's Minister*
Toney Upton, *Connections and Community Pastor*
Johnathon Valdez, *Student Pastor*

The mission of Central Bible Church is "Making God known by making disciples who are changed by God to change their world." We are a Kingdom-minded church committed to training leaders and laypeople through the surrender of all our resources. Your purchase of this book provides spiritual growth resources like this to others who are unable to afford them. If you believe this book would encourage your spiritual walk, but cannot afford it, we will gladly give you a copy.

To request discounts on bulk copies or to make a contribution to our local and global leadership training, please contact us:

centralpress@wearecentral.org.

Learn more about the ministry of Central Bible Church online at www.wearecentral.org.

Central Bible Church
8001 Anderson Boulevard
Fort Worth, Texas 76120
817-274-1315

Made in USA - Kendallville, IN
68141_9798811439805